The Dead Sea Scrolls

The Dead

*Catalog of the Exhibition of Scrolls
and Artifacts from the Collections
of the Israel Antiquities Authority at
the Public Museum of Grand Rapids*

With Original Essays by
Emanuel Tov, James VanderKam,
Pnina Shor and Lena Libman,
Ruth Peled and Ayala Sussmann,
and Bastiaan Van Elderen

Edited by
Ellen Middlebrook Herron

Sea Scrolls

Public Museum of Grand Rapids

William B. Eerdmans Publishing Company
Grand Rapids, Michigan / Cambridge, U.K.

Catalog of the Exhibition of Scrolls and Artifacts from the Collections
of the Israel Antiquities Authority at the Public Museum of Grand
Rapids – Van Andel Museum Center, 16 February – 1 June 2003

Published jointly 2003 by
The Public Museum of Grand Rapids
www.grmuseum.org
and by
Wm. B. Eerdmans Publishing Co.
255 Jefferson Ave. S.E., Grand Rapids, Michigan 49503/
P.O. Box 163, Cambridge CB3 9PU U.K.
www.eerdmans.com

Printed in the United States of America

07 06 05 04 03   7 6 5 4 3 2 1

ISBN 0-8028-2122-7

A list of acknowledgments and photo credits appears on page 140.

To avoid specific religious connotations, the abbreviations BCE (Before the
Common Era) and CE (Common Era) have been used instead of BC (Before
Christ) and AD (*anno Domini*, Latin for "in the year of our Lord").

Contents

Israel Antiquities Authority Director's Statement

Shuka Dorfman
Director General
Israel Antiquities Authority

Hidden for almost 2000 years in remote caves in the Judean Desert, the Dead Sea Scrolls are regarded as the greatest archaeological find of the 20th century. At the end of 2001, the Israel Antiquities Authority (IAA) formally announced the completion of the scientific publication of these sacred and historical manuscripts.

Since its establishment, the IAA has promoted and supported an intense research and publication program headed by Prof. Emanuel Tov from the Hebrew University with a team of over eighty scholars. Along with the promotion of the publication, the IAA established a conservation laboratory dedicated to the preservation of these outstanding 2000 year old manuscripts for future generations.

Another major objective the IAA has undertaken over the past decade is to enable the presentation of the scrolls to the public without endangering their preservation. Although the Dead Sea Scrolls were uncovered more than half a century ago, they still generate unrivalled interest among scholars and laymen alike.

The scrolls, biblical and sectarian, were written as early as the third century BCE, but most date to the first century BCE and the first century CE. They contain fragments of all of the books of the Hebrew Bible (with the exception of the Book of Esther) as well as a complete text of Isaiah. Especially significant are the fragments of the Apocrypha, previously known only in Greek and Latin. The scrolls preserve the Hebrew and Aramaic original versions. The sectarian texts reflect the beliefs and apocalyptic expectations of the community that wrote them.

This exhibition and catalog relate the story of the scrolls' discovery and illuminate their historical and archaeological context. We have chosen twelve scrolls — some more substantial in size, others merely fragments. The scroll texts are accompanied by transcriptions, translations and explanations. Various theories concerning the nature of the Qumran community, its identity and theology are explored also via the selection of archaeological artifacts excavated in Qumran and its environs in the Judean Desert. Light is shed on the nature and working methods of archaeologists, historians, paleographers and conservators.

This exhibition is the product of a fruitful collaboration between the Public Museum of Grand Rapids and the Israel Antiquities Authority. Special thanks are due to its initiator, Weston Fields, head of the Dead Sea Scrolls Foundation, Timothy Chester, Director of Public Museum of Grand Rapids, and Ellen Middlebrook Herron, Guest Curator, who enthusiastically orchestrated the project.

Foreword

Director, Public Museum of Grand Rapids

History is often made and recorded through the acts of anonymous individuals — the product of daily labor that survives beyond their time and place to resonate throughout the ages. So it is with the unknown scribes working 2000 years ago in the religious community of Qumran in the Judean Desert, laboriously copying sacred writing and secular texts onto carefully prepared scrolls made of parchment and papyrus. Stored in pottery jars and carefully secreted away in remote desert caves high above the Dead Sea, these documents rested in solitude for two millennia, enduring the ravages of time to survive and be rediscovered in our own age. Known today as the Dead Sea Scrolls, this archive of documents speaks to us with eloquence and power of moral and social values that continue to define Western civilization.

As the study, translation, conservation and interpretation of the Dead Sea Scrolls progresses, and interest in them intensifies, the Public Museum of Grand Rapids, Michigan is honored to collaborate with the Israel Antiquities Authority in organizing a major exhibition on the subject. *The Dead Sea Scrolls* exhibits original scroll fragments and related archaeological materials in an interpretive context, utilizing the best understanding of current scholarship to explore when the scrolls were written, by whom, and for what purpose. The sometimes conflicting views regarding their meaning are also presented and explored in a manner that respects the universal values embodied in these ancient manuscripts.

The presentation of *The Dead Sea Scrolls* at the Van Andel Museum Center's Lacks Changing Exhibitions Gallery represents a special moment in the 148 year history of the Public Museum of Grand Rapids. Established in 1854 as an educational institution, the Public Museum has a distinguished history of organizing and presenting exceptional interpretive exhibitions of original artifacts that have special relevancy for the citizens it serves. The completion in 1994 of the Public Museum's fifth home, Van Andel Museum Center, ensured that the museum could meet the highest standards for protecting and conserving its own collections and for hosting international loan exhibitions.

The Public Museum of Grand Rapids has been fortunate in enjoying the enthusiastic support of its community and our Israeli colleagues in the development of this exhibition. The generous participation and assistance of Mr. Shuka Dorman, Director General of the Israel Antiquities Authority, and the professionalism and enthusiasm of Guest Curator Ellen Middlebrook Herron and Pnina Shor, Director of the Artifacts Treatment and Conservation Department of the IAA, have been the foundation of the project's success from concept to reality. The IAA's curatorial and conservation staff worked diligently on our behalf and special thanks is due to Hava Katz and Ruth Peled. Special gratitude is given to Weston Fields, Director of the Dead Sea Scrolls Foundation in Jerusalem for suggesting the collaboration and encouraging its progress. The clarity and substance of this catalog have their origins in the fine curatorial work of the Israel Antiquities Authority, the rigorous scholarship of Dr. Emanuel Tov, Professor of the Bible at Hebrew University in Jerusalem, and the guiding hand of guest curator Ellen Middlebrook Herron. Its beauty and existence is the generous gift of the guidance, labor, financial support and skill of William B. Eerdmans Publishing Co. of Grand Rapids. The wonderful learning programs and opportunities that accompany the exhibition were envisioned and planned by museum educator Mary Ellen Munley with the assistance of talented storyteller Syd Lieberman. Jim Muller, Skip Luyk, Neal Bierling, Ruth Oldenburg, Clarence Menninga and Elizabeth Gilson provided special assistance. The Public Museum is especially grateful for the guiding grace and wisdom of Dr. Bastiaan Van Elderen, Professor Emeritus of New Testament Studies at Calvin Theological Seminary. His good humor and delight in bringing this exhibition to Grand Rapids sustained all that labored with him.

A project as complex as *The Dead Sea Scrolls* requires the commitment of government officials and private citizens who expend their time, energy and resources to ensure that the project succeeds. Of particular note has been the support of the Honorable John H. Logie, Mayor of Grand Rapids, and City Manager Kurt F. Kimball. The Museum also recognizes the continuing support of Grand Rapids City Commissioners Scott Bowen, the Rev. Robert Dean, James Jendrasiak, Lynn Rabaut, Roy Schmidt, and Rick Tormala. The Honorable Vernon Ehlers, representing Grand Rapids in the United States Congress, has given freely of his support. Mr. Larry Shay, current president of the Museum's governing board and Mr. Steele A. Taylor, its vice president, have enthusiastically supported every aspect of the exhibition along with fellow trustees John W. Bergstrom, William Foster, Carol Greenburg, Earle S. "Win" Irwin, and Lyman Parks, Jr. The presidents of the museum's two previous support organizations, Ellen Brown of the Public Museum Foundation of Grand Rapids and Jan Thompson of the Friends of the Public Museum have helped to generate the community involvement that is the measure of the exhibition's success.

The President of the newly merged Public Museum of Grand Rapids Friends Foundation, Mr. Dale Robertson, has worked tirelessly to recruit community leadership in support of this initiative. As chair of the committee that directed the gala festivities organized in conjunction with the exhibition's opening, he was ably assisted by Marge Byington, Glenn Borre, John Dean, Barb Groat, Mary Lu Herzog, Robin Keith, Kathy Snyder, Steele Taylor, Jim Tideman, Linda VanderJagt and Jan Thompson. Blue Cross/Blue Shield of Michigan and Steelcase, Inc. both provided significant in-kind support, as did Grand Rapids Community College, Grand Valley State University, Fruitbasket/ Flowerland, Guilford of Maine, West Michigan Piano, St. Cecilia Music Society Youth Choirs, the Western Jazz Quartet, Schubert Male Chorus, artist Stephen Duren and pianist Philip Pletcher. We express deep gratitude to Northern Trust Bank for its key sponsorship of opening events.

Possibilities and dreams require financial support to become reality. The exhibition and its accompanying programs have received major sponsorship from the Jay & Betty Van Andel Foundation, William B. Eerdmans Publishing Co., Public Museum of Grand Rapids Friends Foundation, Grand Rapids Downtown Development Authority, The Gerber Foundation, Steelcase Foundation, WZZM 13, Meijer, Northern Trust Bank, National Endowment for the Arts, Blue Cross/Blue Shield of Michigan, Fifth Third Bank, Star 105.7FM, Wood Newsradio 1300, Steelcase, Inc., and Zondervan. Additional support was received from Grand Valley State University, Calvin College, Irwin Seating Co., Warner, Norcross & Judd, Varnum, Riddering, Schmidt & Howlett, Midwest Safety, URS Corporation, Huntington Private Banking, Monaghan & Associates, Steele A. and Mary Taylor, the City of Grand Rapids IT Department, the Jewish Federation of Grand Rapids, Alticor, Inc. the Louis & Helen Padnos Foundation, and David & Carol Van Andel. This exhibition is supported by an indemnity from the Federal Council on the Arts and the Humanities. Annual support of the activities and programs of the Public Museum of Grand Rapids is made in part by the City of Grand Rapids, the Michigan Council for Arts & Cultural Affairs, a partner agency of the National Endowment for the Arts, the Institute of Museum & Library Services, a federal agency, the Grand Rapids/Kent County Urban Cooperation Board and many private donors.

Finally, any museum is measured by two key assets: its collections and staff. The Public Museum of Grand Rapids is fortunate in having a staff marked by excellence and dedication. I particularly want to note the work of Kay A. Zuris, Assistant Museum Director; Mary Esther Lee, Planning and Development Officer; Thomas Bantle, Curator of Exhibits; Marilyn Merdzinski, Collections and Registration Manager; Christian G. Carron, Chief Curator for Collections; Deidra Mayweather, Public Relations & Marketing Manager; David DeBruyn, Chief Curator, Roger B. Chaffee Planetarium; Paula Gangopadhyay, Curator of Education; Robert Vandermeer, Facility Use Manager; Elizabeth Ricker, Museum Retail Sales Manager; Kerry Sitar, Administrative Analyst; Sam Wiltheiss, Museum Facilties Operations Manager and Randy Rysdyk, Museum Security Manager. Additional staff members who worked directly on this project's success are Ray Baas, Gina Bivins, Trina Burdick, Mary Ann Cheney, Linda Crandall, Pete Daly, Fred DeBoer, David Dennet, Dianne Flynn, Gordie Froman, Jeff Gummere, Shannon Harris, Jennifer Hudson, Veronica Kandl, Jeanne Larsen, Joyce Makinen, Terri Mawhinney, Anne McIntyre, Paula Nelson, Dennis O'Connell, Karen Patterson, Mark Perkins, Cheryl Powell, Ilene Skinner, Linda Sweigart, Peggy Thiel, Janet Thompson-Rea, Gary Tomlinson, RT Tompkins, Maridell VanderBaan, Roger Van Till, Deborah Washburn, Karen Wilburn, Mary Wisnewski, and Mary Wood. Many others undertook work that kept museum operations running smoothly during the planning of the exhibition. While space prohibits the naming of them all, their contributions are all valued and appreciated.

The most important reward for the many individuals and organizations that made *The Dead Sea Scrolls* possible will be the appreciation of students, scholars, and visitors who will tour the exhibition, partake of the rich array of accompanying educational programs and study and enjoy this catalog for years to come.

Preface

Ellen Middlebrook Herron
Guest Curator
The Dead Sea Scrolls

As I was writing the label text for this exhibition, I found that researching the scrolls and learning their story was not the most difficult task I was to face. After months of putting together the facts and stories about the scrolls, one final job remained — writing the last label. Every exhibition should provide visitors with an interesting and educational experience. The material must be interpreted and presented in an understandable way that that makes each visit worthwhile. But I have always felt that the parting message of any exhibition is perhaps the most important. The curator must decide how to sum up the experience and convey the seminal thought that should accompany the visitor back into the world. Some concluding labels are funny, some profound, and occasionally a final message can take what was a perfectly understandable exhibition and leave the visitor hopelessly confused.

I wrote my closing label many times, coming at it from various angles. For weeks I drove my car, ate breakfast, and walked my dog distractedly, constantly asking myself questions to try to discover what I hoped visitors would ponder as they left this exhibition: Should I try to sum up the historical meaning of the scrolls? Could I presume to do that better than the scrolls scholars who have already written so eloquently on the subject? Should I write about their biblical significance? If

I focus on that, how does that impact the message for people who do not hold the Hebrew Bible as their sacred text? Should I speak mostly about the conservation of the scrolls? Scholarship? How the Essenes compare to some modern religious group? I composed, deleted, erased and tore up more words than I wrote for the entire rest of the exhibition. But nothing hit quite the right note.

Then I started to think about what it was about the scrolls that had made the greatest impact upon me while I was researching and writing. This story is exceptionally rich and complex, and it has touched me in many different ways. The plight of the conservation of the scrolls has become an issue very close to my heart. The fact that the scrolls were hidden 2,000 years ago when the Jewish nation was conquered and then found again on the eve of its rebirth has led me to examine my beliefs about predestination and fate. The corroboration that the biblical text (upon which all translations of the Hebrew Bible have been based) is almost exactly the same as it was at the time of the formation of rabbinic Judaism, and the birth of Christianity, has a particular resonance for me.

As this catalog goes to press in early 2003, it is difficult even to name the region in which the scrolls were composed, hidden and found without offending someone. The monikers "Middle East,"

"Israel," "Palestine," "Near East," and "Holy Land" all have unique connotations for different factions. This geographical area has singular significance for numerous groups of people, and few areas of the world can chronicle such a continuously turbulent history. When the scrolls were hidden, Jerusalem and the Jewish nation were being conquered. When the scrolls were rediscovered, a new Jewish nation was born into great violence. In between, conflicts between Christians, Muslims and Jews were recurrent. Today, fierce clashes over territorial rights are commonplace and have peppered the years between 1947 and now.

Amidst mounting political tensions, I realized that what has affected me the most during my study of the scrolls is what I wrote about at the end of the exhibition text. While I knew that Christianity and Judaism shared a common heritage, I was unaware of how intricately linked these two religions are to Islam. Though each religion has developed divergent beliefs and traditions, at their core, they share an historical background. I have often looked at the Middle East "situation" and felt that the factions involved were so hopelessly different that no consensus could ever be reached. Divergent beliefs, conflicting customs and opposing perspectives have made it appear that the only commonalities these groups share are bitterness, anger, and commitment to their side of the struggle. And so it was with wonder that throughout my research, I frequently found ways in which Judaism, Christianity and Islam are alike. While traditions have diverged and the three religions struggle to find any common ground, learning about the scrolls in the context of the time period in which they were created has convinced me there are more commonalities that unite them than many would think.

The Dead Sea Scrolls provide a window into one of the most crucial time periods in the formation of the cultures and traditions of these three great faiths. Collectively, many of us can trace the origins of our legal heritage, social mores, societal models, and religious stories to the time and place of the Dead Sea Scrolls. They were deposited in the caves to save them from violence; they were rediscovered during a time of struggle; and the early days of their study were marked by interfaith and intercultural discord. But the scrolls have somehow inspired academics to see past personal and political differences to work together. Modern day scrolls research is characterized by close cooperation between scholars from many faiths and nations. The product of these labors would be wanting without the talents and diverse perspectives of all of these people. They have come together to work on these documents that are of inestimable value to us all. Perhaps the true legacy of the Dead Sea Scrolls is their power to bring people together.

Thanks

This project has been very special for me to work on, particularly because I was able to bring the scrolls to my home region. West Michigan is a unique area whose people will appreciate experiencing the scrolls firsthand as a community in a way that is perhaps impossible in a larger urban setting. Response from businesses and individuals has been overwhelmingly positive, and it is due to this support that this project was able to come to fruition.

Throughout the process of organizing *The Dead Sea Scrolls,* there have been key people who were absolutely crucial to its success. Many are thanked in Timothy Chester's foreword. There are certain people, however, to whom I would like to extended my gratitude. Dr. Weston Fields of the Dead Sea Scrolls Foundation first approached me about exhibiting the scrolls in the spring of 2001. Thank you, Weston, for opening this world to me and for your guidance through the project. Timothy Chester, Director of the Public Museum of Grand Rapids, has exhibited an enormous amount of courage, fortitude, patience and leadership from the first day that we spoke together about the possibility of mounting this exhibition. We have depended upon each other through the last two years, and I feel that we have formed an excellent professional relationship as well as a strong friendship. Mary Ellen Munley was the educational consultant on the project. In her I found a dedicated, creative professional who encouraged and inspired me, as well as a new friend.

Emanuel Tov, James VanderKam, and Jodi Magness have all generously shared their knowledge and expertise about the scrolls throughout this process. They are three of the most respected Dead Sea Scrolls scholars in the world, and their input has been invaluable. I cannot estimate how much email each of them answered from me dispensing advice, guidance, and correcting my mistakes or misperceptions. They are also the expert voices on the audio tour that accompanies the exhibition, and each is a key participant in our educational programming. I am grateful to all of you for sharing your time and helping to make the information delivered to visitors more accurate.

The entire staff of the Public Museum of Grand Rapids has my respect and gratitude. They have demonstrated throughout the preparation of this exhibition that they are a first-rate, professional team. Their talent, dedication, support and creativity are unmatched.

Great thanks are also due to Wm. B. Eerdmans Publishing Co. of Grand Rapids, Michigan, who published this catalog as a gift to the museum and the community. I especially appreciate the professionalism and patience of Bill and Anita Eerdmans, Claire VanderKam and Klaas Wolterstorff. It is a beautiful volume, with design and layout by Kevin van der Leek. I am proud to have been a part of its production.

I cannot write this without thanking my husband, Joseph, who jumped off a cliff with me when I left my job to pursue this exhibition. His support, faith in me, patience with what seems like interminable absence from home, and his love are what have sustained and inspired me throughout. I couldn't ask for a better partner and best friend.

I have saved the two people that I want to thank the most for last. In the summer of 2001, two representatives from the Israel Antiquities Authority (IAA) came to West Michigan to consider exhibiting the scrolls here. Ruth Peled, with whom I enjoyed working very much, unfortunately retired before this project was completed. Her colleague, Pnina Shor, was the other visitor during that long weekend. As curator of the exhibit on behalf of the IAA, Pnina has personally and patiently led me through the process of presenting the Dead Sea Scrolls in an accurate, interesting way. She has encyclopedic knowledge about the scrolls that she shared with me willingly. Mounting this exhibition has not always been an easy process, but

Pnina has helped to make it very rewarding for me. Through our work together, I have gained not only a valued colleague, but also a treasured new friend.

Lastly, I would like to offer my most sincere thanks to Prof. Bastiaan Van Elderen. Bas and I have worked together since 1996 on various projects, and I was thrilled when he agreed to advise me on *The Dead Sea Scrolls*. When I requested his help, I had no idea how much I was asking of him. Bas has worked tirelessly on almost every aspect of this exhibition, from research to label text to educational activities to promotion — and everything in between. He has generously shared his vast knowledge with me and with all from the museum who have asked for his help. Without his guidance, nothing about this project would be as good as it is. Thank you, Bas, for everything. You are a respected mentor, a priceless asset to the community, and a cherished friend. We couldn't have done this without you.

Please note that this volume was adapted from an out-of-print catalog that accompanied an exhibition of the same scrolls and objects lent by the Israel Antiquities Authority at the Art Gallery of New South Wales in Sydney, Australia, in 2000. The text in the present catalog describing the specific scrolls and artifacts on display was composed by Ruth Peled and Ayala Sussmann of the

IAA (except where otherwise indicated). As editor, I occasionally altered their text for an American audience, but the substance of the descriptions is their work. In addition, the transcriptions and translations of all non-biblical scrolls were taken from Florentino García-Martínez and Eibert J.C. Tigchelaar's, *The Dead Sea Scrolls Study Edition,* published by Wm. B. Eerdmans Publishing Co. in Grand Rapids, Michigan. Biblical transcriptions are from the *Discoveries in the Judaean Desert* series, with translations by Bastiaan Van Elderen. References can be found on the description page for each scroll. In addition, Prof. Van Elderen composed the glossary and collaborated with me on the select bibliography.

Introduction

Bastiaan T. Van Elderen
Professor Emeritus
Vrije Universiteit, Amsterdam

The discovery of the Dead Sea Scrolls has frequently and rightly been described as the greatest archaeological discovery in the 20th century. Little did Muhammed ed-Dhib, the Bedouin discoverer of the first cave with its scrolls in the late 1940's, realize the worldwide impact that this discovery would have. Biblical studies throughout the world have been significantly influenced by the Dead Sea Scrolls as scholars gained new insights and perspectives in the study of Second Temple Judaism and the context in which Christianity arose. Hence, an opportunity to see some of the documents and related artifacts, over 2000 years old, is a moving experience.

As more caves in the area along the northwest shore of the Dead Sea yielded manuscripts, the question arose whether the scrolls were related to Khirbet Qumran, a complex of ruins on a plateau nearby. These ruins, covering an area about 250 × 300 feet, were excavated in the 1950's under the direction of Father Roland de Vaux, director of the École Biblique et Archéologique Française in Jerusalem. On the basis of his archaeological work at the site, de Vaux concluded that the ruins of Khirbet Qumran were those of a religious community and that the scrolls and the excavated area are directly related. Not only are many of the caves (#4, 5, 7, 8, 9, 10) located near the ruins, but practices alluded to in the scrolls are demonstrable in the communal buildings. This interpretation of the site and the scrolls, although not universally accepted, is the prevailing interpretation among biblical scholars.

Almost every sectarian movement in first century Judaism has been identified with the Qumran community — the Pharisees, the Sadducees, the Zealots, the Essenes, and even a Jewish-Christian sect. Scholarly consensus generally identifies the Qumran people as a modified form of the Essenes as described by Flavius Josephus, Pliny the Elder, and Philo of Alexandria. The community was a communal society to which the members gave their possessions upon admission. Membership was through an admission process involving a two-year probation period which was strictly monitored by the superiors. The facilities in the community, as uncovered in the excavations, were for the collective services of the community and not for individual or personal use. The members lived outside the communal buildings in tents and caves and gathered in the main building for common meals, rituals, worship and other communal activities. From the size of these facilities it is thought that the community consisted of about 200 members at a given time.

Various criteria, including numismatics, pottery, paleography, linguistics, and Carbon 14, date the scrolls between the late 3rd century BCE and the

1st century CE. Included in the library of some 900 manuscripts, many fragmentary, are over 200 biblical manuscripts which are over a thousand years older than previously known major copies of the Hebrew Bible. As a result, there have been some significant improvements in establishing the text of the Hebrew Bible. The size and antiquity of this discovery are remarkable and unparalleled.

Included in the collection are also some apocryphal and pseudepigraphical books from the Second Temple Period (520 BCE – 70 CE) and sectarian literature which describes the Qumran community and its motivation for being in the desert. These Jews had become dissatisfied with religious conditions in Jerusalem and had withdrawn to the desert to await the coming of the Messiah who would lead them as an army to Jerusalem to set up the Messianic Kingdom there. While waiting for the sudden arrival of the Messiah, the community kept itself in a state of readiness through various rituals and lustrations described in the sectarian literature and reflected in the various installations in the ruins. This literature provides a window into first century Judaism, the matrix in which Christianity arose and the seeds for the later rise of Islam were sown.

The most mysterious and puzzling document in the Qumran Library is the Copper Scroll found in Qumran Cave 3. Inscribed on the two rolls of copper is an Aramaic text which describes and locates the hiding places of various treasures between Jerusalem and the Dead Sea. Although none of these treasures has been recovered, scholarly opinion is divided regarding the origin and nature of these treasures – possessions of the members of the community, treasures from the Jerusalem temple before its destruction in 70 CE, or other treasures of the community hidden for security reasons?

The publication and study of the scrolls have been plagued by the political tensions in the Middle East. Conditions in Palestine in the late 1940's resulted in the transfer to the United States of four scrolls from Qumran Cave 1. Three of these scrolls were published by the American Schools of Oriental Research, then centered at Yale University. Subsequently these scrolls were advertised in the Wall Street Journal in 1954 and purchased by the Hebrew University in Jerusalem, and are now housed in the Shrine of the Book in Jerusalem with the other three scrolls originally discovered by the Bedouin shepherd boy. Other scrolls, especially from the large cache found in Cave 4, were housed in the Rockefeller Museum in East Jerusalem. A small international team was organized to publish these scrolls. The political change brought about by the Six-Day War in 1967, in which Israel gained occupation of East Jerusalem, necessitated the reorganization of this international team. This occasioned some confusion and consequently further delay in the publication process.

In addition, the publication was hampered by the limited number of scholars assigned to analyze the materials and to the tedious process of identifying fragments. Impatience in the scholarly world resulted in the reorganization of the publication team in the early 1990's. Prof. Emanuel Tov, Professor of Bible at Hebrew University, Jerusalem, was appointed editor-in-chief of *Discoveries in the Judaean Desert (DJD),* the official publication of the Dead Sea Scrolls. Within a decade Prof. Tov, with a team of some 50 international scholars, published almost all of the Qumran texts. Volume 39 (Introduction and Indexes) appeared in 2002. Prof. Tov details his experiences as editor-in-chief in his essay in this catalog.

The preservation of the Qumran ruins has been an on-going problem for archaeologists. Some features of the exposed ruins of Khirbet Qumran are disintegrating (e.g., a staircase intact in 1962 is rubble today). Likewise, the proper conservation of manuscripts is a real concern to scholars. In the case of the Dead Sea Scrolls, techniques and procedures employed in the 1950's in some cases have damaged rather than preserved the manuscripts. New techniques and procedures are being used today to rescue the scrolls from further damage. In their essay in this catalog, Head of the Artifacts Treatment and Conservation Department at the Israel Antiquities Authority, Pnina Shor, and Lena Libman, the IAA's Head of the Conservation Laboratory of the Dead Sea Scrolls, describe how the scrolls have been treated in the past fifty years and the current "state of the art" of manuscript preservation being applied to the scrolls today.

Throughout history human beings have used various systems to measure time and to reconcile the lunar calendar with the solar calendar. As a result of the divergent systems used in antiquity, it is difficult to date some events precisely, such as the year of the Exodus of the Israelites from Egypt, or the year of the birth of Jesus. Like their contemporaries, the Qumran community was concerned about chronology and the dating of its various feasts. The Dead Sea Scrolls include a number of calendrical texts, such as Calendrical Document 4Q325, displayed in the exhibit and described on pages 70-73 of this catalog. Prof. James VanderKam at the University of Notre Dame has specialized in the study of these calendrical texts from Qumran. In his essay in this catalog, he reviews the the contributions of the Dead Sea Scrolls to this complex problem of ancient chronologies.

This exhibit includes examples of the various genera of literature found in the Qumran library.

There are biblical texts (one in the ancient paleo-Hebrew script), biblical commentary, sectarian texts describing the community, liturgical texts, and non-canonical texts. Artifacts from the ruins and the caves reflect the everyday existence of the Qumran people. The legends accompanying the items will meaningfully interpret the materials for the viewer. Even this small portion of the extensive Dead Sea Scrolls library and objects from Qumran will demonstrate the importance of this discovery for biblical and historical studies of 1st century Palestine, for students of the history of the formation of Western society and culture, and for insight into the foundations of the three great monotheistic religions of Judaism, Christianity and Islam. Given these important contributions to various disciplines, the historical cultural, and religious significance of the Dead Sea Scrolls ranks their discovery as the greatest in the 20th century.

Treasures from the Judean Desert

Ruth Peled
Director of Special Projects
Israel Antiquities Authority

Ayala Sussmann
Director of Publications
Israel Antiquities Authority

Ancient Hebrew scrolls that were accidentally discovered in 1947 in the Judean Desert by a Bedouin boy have kindled popular enthusiasm as well as serious scholarly interest over the past half a century. The source of this excitement is what these Dead Sea Scrolls reveal about the history of the Second Temple Period (520 BCE-70 CE), particularly from the second century BCE until the destruction of the Second Temple in 70 CE, a time of crucial developments in the crystallization of the monotheistic religions.

One discovery led to another, and 11 scroll-yielding caves and a habitation site eventually were uncovered. Since 1947, the site of these discoveries — the Qumran region (the desert plain and the adjoining mountainous ridge) and the Qumran site — have been subjected to countless searches. The first trove found by the Bedouin in the Judean Desert consisted of seven large scrolls from what is now called Cave 1. The unusual circumstances of the find, on the eve of Israel's War of Independence, obstructed the initial negotiations for the purchase of all the scrolls. Shortly before the establishment of the State of Israel, Professor E.L. Sukenik of the Hebrew University acquired three of the scrolls from a Christian Arab antiquities dealer in Bethlehem. The remaining four scrolls reached the hands of Mar Athanasius Yeshua Samuel, Metropolitan of the Syrian Jacobite Monastery of

St. Mark in Jerusalem. In 1949, he traveled to the United States with the scrolls, but five years went by before the prelate found a purchaser.

On June 1, 1954, Mar Samuel placed an advertisement in The Wall Street Journal offering "The Four Dead Sea Scrolls" for sale. The advertisement was brought to the attention of Professor Sukenik's son, Yigael Yadin, who had recently retired as chief of staff of the Israel Defense Forces and reverted to his primary vocation, archaeology. With the aid of intermediaries, the four scrolls were purchased from Mar Samuel for US$250,000. The scrolls that had eluded the father were now at the son's disposal.

The seven scrolls from Cave 1, now on exhibit to the public in the Shrine of the Book in Jerusalem's Israel Museum, are Isaiah A, Isaiah B, the Habakkuk Commentary, the Thanksgiving Scroll, the Community Rule (or the Manual of Discipline), the War Rule (or the War of the Sons of Light Against the Sons of Darkness) and the Genesis Apocryphon, the last being in Aramaic.

Archaeological Investigations

The Caves At least a year elapsed between the discovery of the scrolls in 1947 and the initiation of a systematic archaeological investigation of the Qumran region. The northern Dead Sea area, the location of Qumran, became and remained part of

Jordan until 1967. The search for scroll material rested in the hands of the Bedouin, who ravaged the Cave 1 site. Early in 1949, the cave site was finally identified by the archaeological authorities of Jordan. The director of the Jordanian Antiquities Department, G. Lankester Harding, undertook to excavate Cave 1 with Père Roland de Vaux, a French Dominican priest who headed the École Biblique in Jerusalem. Exploration of the cave, which lay a kilometer north of Wadi Qumran, yielded at least 70 fragments, including bits of the original seven scrolls. This discovery established the provenance of the purchased scrolls. Also recovered were archaeological artifacts that confirmed the scroll dates suggested by paleographic study. The Bedouin continued to search for scrolls, as these scraps of leather proved to be a fine source of income. Because Cave 1 had been exhausted by the archaeological excavation, the fresh material that the Bedouin were offering proved that Cave 1 was not an isolated phenomenon in the desert and that other caves with manuscripts also existed. The years between 1951 and 1956 were marked by accelerated activity in both the search for caves and the archaeological excavation of sites related to the manuscripts. An eight-kilometer-long strip of cliffs was thoroughly investigated. Of the 11 caves that yielded manuscripts, five were discovered by the Bedouin and six by archaeologists.

Some of the caves were particularly rich in material. Cave 3 preserved two oxidized rolls of beaten copper (the Copper Scroll), containing a lengthy list of real or imaginary hidden treasures — a tantalizing enigma to this day. In Cave 4, 15,000 fragments from at least 600 composite texts were found. Cave 11, the last manuscript cave discovered, in 1956, provided extensive documents, including the Psalms Scroll (pp. 94-97 of this catalog), an Aramaic Targum of Job, and the Temple Scroll. Yigael Yadin acquired the Temple Scroll in 1967; it is now housed with the first seven scrolls in the Shrine of the Book at the Israel Museum. All the remaining manuscripts — sizable texts, as well as minute fragments — are stored in the premises of the Israel Antiquities Authority.

Khirbet Qumran (The Qumran Ruin) De Vaux gradually realized the need to identify a habitation site close to the caves. Excavating such a site could provide clues that would help to identify the people who deposited the scrolls.

The ruins of Qumran lie on a barren terrace between the limestone cliffs of the Judean Desert and the bed of a fossil lake along the Dead Sea. The excavations uncovered a complex of structures, 80 × 100 meters, preserved to a considerable height. De Vaux regarded the structures as neither military not private but rather communal in character. Nearby were remains of burials. Pottery uncovered was identical to that found in Cave 1 and confirmed the link with the nearby caves.

Following the initial excavations, de Vaux suggested that this site was the wilderness retreat established by the Essene sect, which was alluded to by ancient historians. The sectarians inhabited neighboring locations, most likely caves, tents and solid structures, but depended on the center for such communal facilities as stores of food and water. Excavations conducted in 1956 and 1958 at the neighboring site of Ein Feshkha proved it to be the agricultural adjunct of Qumran.

Dating of the Scrolls The discovery of the Dead Sea Scrolls caused heated controversy in scholarly circles over their age and the identity of the community they represented.

Professor Sukenik, after initially defining the provenance of the scrolls as the Second Temple Period, recognized their special significance and advocated the theory that they were remnants of the library of the Essenes. At that time, however, he was vociferously opposed by a number of scholars who doubted the authenticity of the texts. Today, scholarly opinion regarding the timespan and background of the Dead Sea Scrolls is anchored in historical, paleographic and linguistic evidence, corroborated firmly by carbon-14 dat-

ings. Some manuscripts were written and copied in the third century BCE, but the bulk of the material, particularly the texts that reflect on a sectarian community, are originals or copies form the first century BCE; a number of texts date from as late as the years preceding the destruction of the site, in 68 CE, at the hands of the Roman legions.

The Essenes

The origins of the Qumran sect are thought by some to be in the communities of the Hasidim, the pious anti-Hellenistic circles formed in the early days of the Maccabees. The Hasidim may have been the precursors of the Essenes, who were concerned about growing Hellenization and strove to abide by the Torah.

Archaeological and historical evidence indicates that Qumran was founded in the second half of the second century BCE, during the time of the Maccabean dynasty. A hiatus in the occupation of the site is linked to evidence of a huge earthquake. Qumran was abandoned at about the time of the Roman incursion of 68 CE, two years before the collapse of Jewish self-government in Judea and the destruction of the Temple in Jerusalem in 70 CE.

The chief sources of information for the history of this fateful timespan are the Qumran scrolls and the excavations, but earlier information on the Essenes was provided by their contemporaries:

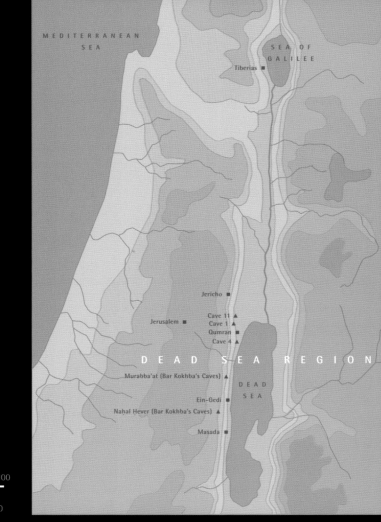

MEDITERRANEAN
SEA

SEA OF
GALILEE

Tiberias ■

Jericho ■

Cave 11 ▲
Cave 1 ▲
Qumran ■
Cave 4 ▲

Jerusalem ■

D E A D   S E A   R E G I O N

Murabba'at (Bar Kokhba's Caves) ▲

DEAD
SEA

Ein-Gedi ■

Naḥal Ḥever (Bar Kokhba's Caves) ▲

Masada ■

meters		feet
1000		3281
500		1640
200		656
100		328
sea level		0

miles

0   25   50   75   100

0   50   100   150

kilometers

Josephus Flavius, Philo of Alexandria and Pliny the Elder. Their accounts are continuously being borne out by the site excavations and study of the writings.

The historian Josephus relates the division of the Jews of the Second Temple Period into three orders: the Sadducees, the Pharisees and the Essenes. The Sadducees included mainly the priestly and aristocratic families, the Pharisees constituted the lay circles, and the Essenes were a separatist group, part of which formed an ascetic monastic community that retreated to the wilderness. The exact political and religious affinities of each of these groups, as well as their development and interrelationships, are still relatively obscure and are the source of widely disparate scholarly views.

The crisis that brought about the secession of the Essenes from mainstream Judaism is thought to have occurred when the Maccabean ruling princes, Jonathan (160-142 BCE) and Simeon (142-134 BCE), usurped the office of high priest (which included secular duties), much to the consternation of conservative Jews; some of them could not tolerate the situation and denounced the new rulers. The persecution of the Essenes and their leader, the "Teacher of Righteousness," probably elicited the sect's apocalyptic visions. These included the overthrow of the "Wicked Priest" of Jerusalem and of the evil people and, in the dawn of the Messi-anic Age, the recognition of their community as the true Israel. The retreat of these Jews into the desert would enable them "to separate themselves from the congregation of perverse men" (Community Rule 5:2).

A significant feature of the Essene sect is its calendar, which was based on a solar system of 364 days, unlike the common Jewish calendar which was lunar and consisted of 354 days. It is not clear how the sectarian calendar was reconciled, as was the normative Jewish calendar, with the astronomical time system (see Calendrical Document, pp. 70-73). The sectarian calendar was always reckoned from a Wednesday, the day on which God created the luminaries. The year consisted of 52 weeks, divided into four seasons of 13 weeks each, and the festivals consistently fell on the same days of the week. A similar solar system was long familiar from pseudepigraphic works. The sectarian calendar played a weighty role in the schism of the community from the rest of Judaism, as the festivals and fast days of the sect were ordinary workdays for the mainstream community, and vice versa. The author of the Book of Jubilees accuses the followers of the lunar calendar of turning secular "days of impurity" into "festivals and holy days" (Jubilees 6:36-37).

The Essenes persisted in a separatist existence through two centuries, occupying themselves with study and a communal way of life that included worship, prayer and work. It is clear, however, that large groups of adherents also lived in towns and villages outside the Qumran area.

The word "Essene" is never distinctly mentioned in the scrolls. How, then, can we attribute either the writings or the sites of the Judean Desert to the Essenes? The argument in favor of this ascription is supported by the tripartite division of Judaism referred to in Qumran writings (for example, in the Nahum Commentary), into Ephraim, Menasseh and Judah, corresponding to the Pharisees, the Sadducees and the Essenes. As the Essenes refer to themselves in the scrolls as Judah, it is clear who they regarded themselves to be. Moreover, their religious concepts and beliefs as attested in the scrolls conform to those recorded in contemporary writings and stand in sharp contrast to those of the other known Jewish groups.

In most cases, the principles of the Essene way of life and beliefs are described by contemporaneous writers in language similar to the descriptions found in the scrolls. Customs described in ancient sources as Essene — such as the probationary period for new members, the strict hierarchy practiced in the organization of the sect, their frequent ablutions, communal meals — are echoed in the scrolls. Finally, the location of the sect is assigned to the Dead Sea area by the Roman historian, Pliny the Elder.

Diversity of Opinions Although this evidence is accepted by the majority of scholars in identifying the Essenes with the Qumran settlement and the manuscripts found in the surrounding caves, some scholars remain unconvinced. Some propose that the site was a military garrison or even a winter villa. The scrolls are viewed as an eclectic collection, neither necessarily inscribed in the Dead Sea area nor sectarian in nature, perhaps even the remains of the library of the Temple in Jerusalem. Other scholars view the texts as the writings of forerunners or even followers of Jesus — Jewish Christians — who still observed Jewish law.

Ancient sources provide us with diverging reports regarding the living environment of the Essene communities: Philo states that they lived in small villages, Josephus wrote that they were scattered in various settlements, whereas Pliny referred to a separate Essene settlement located near the Dead Sea.

The central structures at the site of Qumran could have functioned as a center for the activities of a community during the day. However, only a small number of individuals could have lived there. Due to finds in the vicinity of the site, it has been surmised by many that most of the community members lived in neighboring caves, tents and huts which were linked to the site by a network of paths.

It is feasible that the isolated location of the Dead Sea would lure such a group as the Essenes, as it represented an eschatological paradise, an abode of purity and a haven where they could cut themselves off from the impure. Only at the End of Days would they return from the desert, "to camp in the Desert of Jerusalem" (War Rule 1:2-3) and wrest Jerusalem from the hands of the wicked.

A sectarian's day began before dawn with the recitation of prayers, hymns and benedictions. Phylacteries found in the excavations (see pp. 74-77, 118) give reason to assume that these were worn during prayers. Meals were communal and probably accompanied by blessings – "They shall eat in common and bless in common and deliberate in common" (Community Rule 6:2-3) – outlining a life reminiscent of a monastic community.

Hardly any mention is made either by historians or in the sect's writings of the daily occupations and livelihood of the inhabitants. It is obvious, however, that such a group would have functioned as self-sufficient unit. True evidence of agriculture comes form the site of Ein Feshkha, a mere three kilometers away. Remains of date pits and palm fronds were found at both sites, as well as in the caves. Recent excavations have also revealed the production of date honey.

Sheep and cattle were raised in the area, as evidenced by the wealth of parchment found, both used and unused. This indicates tannery activity, which can probably be linked to the pools and channels at the site. Pieces of linen and wool, sheep shears, spindle whorls, mats and baskets are all evidence of production of textiles and weaves. A potters' workshop, including a kiln, substantiates the assumption that pottery was produced at the site. Scribal work could have occupied a number of Qumranites, as well – the inkwells recovered are proof of local scribal activity.

No doubt a certain measure of market economy was locally practiced; the large number of coins recovered could represent wages received for work outside the community. Within the community's bounds, a communal ownership of property and means was, no doubt, the rule:

> But when the second year has passed, he shall be examined, and if it be his destiny, according to the judgment of the Congregation, to enter the community, then he shall be inscribed among his brethren in the order of his rank for the Law, and for justice, and for the pure Meal; his property shall be merged and he shall offer his counsel

and judgment to the Community. (Community Rule 6:20-23).

The Qumran Library

The writings recovered in the Qumran environs have restored to us a voluminous corpus of Jewish documents dating from the third century BCE to 68 CE, demonstrating the rich literary activity of Second Temple Period Jewry. The collection comprises varies documents, most of them of a distinct religious bent. The chief categories represented are biblical, apocryphal or pseudepigraphical, and sectarian writings. The study of this original library has demonstrated that the boundaries between these categories are far from clear-cut.

The biblical manuscripts include what are probably the earliest copies of these texts to have come down to us. Most of the books of the Bible are represented in the collection. Some books are extant in a large number of copies; others are represented on scraps of parchment. The biblical texts display considerable similarity to the standard Masoretic (received) Text. This, however, is not always the rule, and many texts diverge from the Masoretic. For example, some of the texts of Samuel from Cave 4 follow the Septuagint, the Greek version of the Bible translated in the third to second centuries BCE. Indeed, Qumran has yielded copies of the Septuagint in Greek.

The biblical scrolls in general have provided many new readings that facilitate the reconstruction of the textual history of the Old Testament. It is also significant that several manuscripts of the Bible, including the Leviticus Scroll, are inscribed not in the Jewish script dominant at the time, but in the ancient paleo-Hebrew script.

A considerable number of apocryphal and pseudepigraphic texts are preserved at Qumran, where original Hebrew and Aramaic versions of these Jewish compositions of the Second Temple Period were first encountered. These writings, which are not included in the canonical Jewish scriptures, were preserved by different Christian churches and transmitted in Greek, Ethiopic, Syriac, Armenian and other translations.

Some of these are narrative texts closely related to biblical compositions, such as the Book of Jubilees and Enoch (pp. 82-85), whereas others are independent works. Apparently, some of these compositions were treated by the Qumran community as canonical and were studied by them.

The most original writings from Qumran are the sectarian ones, which were practically unknown until their discovery in 1947. An exception is the Damascus Document, which lacked a definite identification before the discoveries of the Dead Sea area. This widely varied literature reveals the beliefs and customs of a pietistic commune, probably centered at Qumran, and includes rules and ordinances, biblical commentaries, apocalyptic visions and liturgical works generally attributed to the last quarter of the second century BCE and onwards.

The "rules," collections of rules and instructions reflecting the practices of the commune, are exemplified by the Damascus Document (pp. 50-53), the Community Rule (pp. 54-57), and Some Torah Precepts (pp. 66-69). Here, we witness a considerable corpus of legal material (*halakhah*) that has much in common with the rabbinic tradition preserved at a later date in the Mishnah. The *halakhah* emerging from the sectarian writings seems to be corroborated by the sectarian *halakhah* referred to in rabbinic sources.

The biblical commentaries (*pesharim*), such as the Habakkuk Commentary, the Nahum Commentary (pp. 78-81) and the Hosea Commentary, are attested to solely at Qumran and grew out of the sect's eschatological presuppositions. The Scriptures were scanned by the sect for allusions to current and future events. These allusions could be understood only by the sectarians themselves, because only they possessed "eyes to see" – their distinct eschatological vision. Liturgical works figure prominently among the sectarian manuscripts at Qumran, due to the centrality of prayer in this period. The Thanksgiving psalms (*Hodayot*) are of two types: those characterized by a personal tone, attributed by some to the "Teacher of Righteousness," and the communal types, referring to a group.

Many more compositions deserve mention, but this brief survey demonstrates the major role played by the Dead Sea Scrolls in our understanding of this pivotal moment in Jewish history.

History

First Temple Period	850–586 BCE
Second Temple Period	520 BCE –70 CE
First Jewish Revolt	68–70 CE

Literary Milestones

c. 6th century BCE	Canonization of the Torah (Pentateuch), the first of the 3 major divisions of the Hebrew Bible
c. 4th century BCE	Canonization of the Nevi'im (the Prophets), the second of the 3 major divisions of the Hebrew Bible
c. mid-3rd century BCE	Completion of the Septuagint (translation of the Pentateuch into Greek)
c. 200 BCE – 100 CE	Apocryphal and apocalyptic literature
c. 40–50 CE	Beginnings of the New Testament
c. 90 CE	Canonization of the Ketuvim (Hagiographa), the third of the 3 major divisions of the Hebrew Bible
c. 200 CE	Mishnah (first part of the Talmud) edited by Rabbi Judah the Prince

Authors Who Mention the Essenes and/or Qumran

Philo of Alexandria	c. 30 BCE – 45 CE
Pliny the Elder	c. 23–79 CE
Flavius Josephus	c. 38–100 CE

Political and Military Events

586 BCE	Destruction of Jerusalem by Babylonians under Nebuchadnezzar II; beginning of Babylonian Exile
538 BCE	Return of exiles to Judea permitted by Cyrus the Great of Persia
333 BCE	Alexander the Great extends Greek rule to Palestine and Egypt
323 BCE	Alexander's empire divided into 3 parts: Antigonids in Macedonia; Seleucids in Syria; Ptolemies in Egypt
301 BCE	Ptolemies' rule over Judea begins

Political and Military Events, continued

198 BCE	Seleucids' rule over Judea begins
168 BCE	Hasmonean revolt
164 BCE	Temple purified by Judas Maccabeus
63 BCE	Rome occupies Jerusalem
37 BCE	Herod the Great conquers Jerusalem
6 BCE – 41 CE	Judea, Samaria and Edom placed under procurators
44–66 CE	Rule of the procurators
66 CE	Revolt against Rome
c. 68 CE	Roman legions destroy the Qumran settlement
70 CE	Roman legions conquer Jerusalem and destroy the Temple
73 CE	Masada falls to Rome

Qumran Timeline: Father Roland de Vaux's

Israelite Period	8th–7th centuries BCE
Period Ia	c. 130–100 BCE
Period Ib	c. 100-31 BCE
Break in occupation after earthquake in 31 BCE	
Period II	c. 4 BCE – 68 CE
Period III (Roman)	c. 68–90 CE

Qumran Timeline: Revised by Jodi Magness

Israelite Period	8th–7th centuries BCE
Period Ia	Did not exist
Period Ib	2 Phases
	a) 100-50 BCE - 31 BCE
Short break in occupation after earthquake in 31 BCE	
	b) 31 BCE – 9/8-4 BCE
Period II	c. 4 BCE – 68 CE
Period III (Roman)	68 CE – 73/74 CE

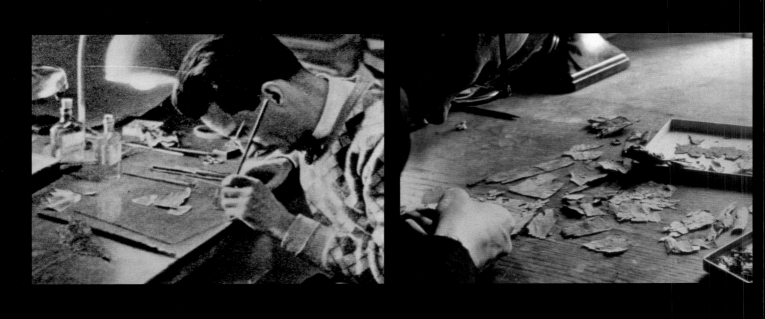

Conservation of the Dead Sea Scrolls

Pnina Shor
Head of Artifacts Treatment and Conservation Department
Israel Antiquities Authority

Lena Libman
Head of Conservation Laboratory of the Dead Sea Scrolls
Israel Antiquities Authority

The conservation and preservation of the Dead Sea Scrolls have concerned both scholars and conservators since their discovery. The removal of the scrolls from the caves in which they had been preserved for over 2000 years put a stop to the environmental stability which had ensured their preservation.

The scrolls revealed in the caves of Qumran are made of both parchment and papyrus. Alongside some large parchment scrolls, thousands of smaller fragments were found, comprising over 1200 plates, 300 of which are made of papyrus.

The ravages of time heavily affected the scrolls from their discovery by the Bedouin shepherd in 1947 until the establishment of the conservation laboratory of the Israel Antiquities Authority in 1991. The work of the laboratory is based on up-to-date conservation methods used worldwide.

In contrast to the academic publication of the scroll texts, which is now formally completed, the task of their conservation and preservation is still ongoing due to their extreme brittleness, and the continuing progress being made in conservation methods.

The first to deal with the preservation of the Dead Sea Scrolls were the scholars — de Vaux, Cross, Milik, Starkey, Strugnell, Allegro and others — who came to the Rockefeller Museum in Jerusalem to study the scrolls soon after their discovery.

While the scholars did their best to prevent damage, their intention was to form a coherent text from fragments which they had identified as being related to each other. Though professional advice regarding preservation techniques was scarce, an effort was made to observe certain basic principles of conservation. Some information came from museums in Europe, particularly from the Vatican Library.

The procedures described by the scholars included brushing the surface of the parchment with a very fine camel-hair brush; treatment of dark stains with castor oil; placing the fragments in a glass humidifier to facilitate their straightening. Related texts were joined with cellotape, which also served as a support on the reverse of the reconstructed manuscripts. The fragments were placed between glass plates which were sealed with adhesive tape.

At this stage, the plates were photographed by the expert photographer of the museum, Najib Albina, who used infra-red and ultraviolet rays for his superb photographs, enabling researchers to proceed with their work abroad and providing a reliable record of the condition of the scrolls and the script shortly after their discovery.

In 1962, H.J. Plenderleith from the British Museum, then director of ICCROM (International Centre for the Study of the Preservation and

Restoration of Cultural Property), was invited to the Rockefeller Museum for consultation on the Ezekiel Scroll. His advice was of relevance for all of the parchment scrolls.

In 1963, in view of plans to mount an exhibition of scrolls abroad, Ms. Valerie Foulkes, a conservator at the British Museum, was invited to assist in selecting and preparing scrolls.

Ms. Foulkes attempted to improve the condition of some of the fragments. She was the first to write a detailed report on the conservation requirements.

The Six-Day War in 1967 marked the transition of the Rockefeller Museum and all of its holdings to the Government of the State of Israel. The Israel Department of Antiquities was appointed custodian of all its collections, including the Dead Sea Scrolls.

When the war broke out, the scrolls were hidden within the building. After the war, once the scrolls had been found, an inventory of over 1200 plates of fragments was compiled. The staff of the Department of Antiquities and the curator of the Shrine of the Book reviewed the condition of the scrolls and their state of preservation. It was now necessary to reverse a combination of destructive factors which had affected the scrolls. The cellotape used to join fragments and cover cracks had caused irreversible damage. The aging of the adhesives and the pressure of the glass caused the edges to gelatinize and the skins to darken, to the extent that some of the texts are no longer legible.

An air-conditioned environment was established, and conservators from the laboratories of the Israel Museum began the lengthy process of removing the glass plates and replacing them with cardboard, as well as removing the cellotape and its residues from the fragments. Rice paper and perspex (plexiglass or lucite) glue provided extra support on the back of the fragments. For storage, fragments were laid on rice paper and placed between plates of cardboard; for exhibition purposes, fragments were stretched between two layers of silk fabric and framed by perspex plates. Once the treatment was completed, the plates were returned to the air-conditioned environment at the Rockefeller building.

In 1991, the Israel Antiquities Authority (formerly the Israel Department of Antiquities) established a conservation laboratory at its premises in the Rockefeller Museum building. Esther Boyd-Alkalay, the expert in paper and parchment conservation in Israel, was asked to assist in a general assessment of the state of preservation and storage of the scrolls and advise on their conservation and preservation.

During the first year under her guidance, the laboratory experimented with different procedures of conservation and preservation of ancient vellum. It was then decided to first remove the parchment from the plain window glass plates and the acidic cardboard which housed them.

Detailed descriptions of the condition of the fragments were recorded, including photography and mapping of each of the fragments, no matter how tiny. Then each fragment was examined under a microscope to check the deterioration and to consolidate delaminated areas. At the same time, an international team of experts sponsored by the Getty Conservation Institute came to Israel and recommended the appropriate methods for conservation of the scrolls.

A united team of scientists researched the damage and changes which affected the scrolls since their discovery. The research included the climatic condition of the caves (relative humidity and temperature) and the causes of physical, chemical and biological deterioration. In the course of the joint project, samples of leather, ink, salt crystals, molds and fungi were examined. The results confirmed that the ink is carbon-based; that the fungi on the scrolls are in a passive state and will remain so as long as the relative humidity does not exceed 60%; and that the scrolls should be stored in a climate-controlled storeroom at a temperature of 20^0 C (68^0 F) and relative humidity of 50%.

The most time-consuming task continues to be the removal of the cellotape which was used as the connecting material in the fifties. After temporary reinforcement of damaged areas with Japanese tissue paper on the recto, or front side, the tape is loosened by a heated surgical scalpel from the verso, or back side. Tape residues and adhesive which have penetrated into the parchment are removed by organic solvents. This procedure, known as poulticing, is repeated until the surface is no longer sticky. Then the verso of the fragment is reinforced wherever necessary with Japanese tissue paper, and the temporary reinforcement is removed from the recto of the parchment. This operation cannot be standardized; each of the thousands of fragments requires individual treatment.

The preserved fragments are then arranged on acid-free cardboard, attached with hinges made of Japanese tissue paper and stored in protective Solander boxes in the climate-controlled storeroom. The treated plates are checked periodically.

When scrolls are being prepared for exhibition, another housing system is devised. The fragments are sewn between two layers of Stabiltex (polyester net) stretched in acid-free mounts (cardboard frames), and enclosed in a frame made of polycarbonate plates.

As far as the parchment plates are concerned, the procedures have proved efficient. Our treatment is reversible so that, if a more advanced method is devised in the future, it will be possible to alter the treatment without causing further damage.

At first it seemed that the state of preservation of papyrus fragments was much better than that of the parchment, because the sticky mass of cellotape adhesive did not penetrate the papyri and remained on its surface. However removing the cellotape from such fibrous material without causing damage proved to be problematic. Also many of the papyri bear text on both sides, and cellotape is glued on the script as well. We have attempted several methods — chemical as well as laser rays — but have not yet found the ideal one.

When mounted for exhibition the papyrus fragments are set within a lacy pattern made of Japanese tissue paper, cut according to the shape of the fragments, and glued with tiny hinges, avoiding the text. The edges of the pattern are then stretched in acid-free mounts and enclosed in a frame made of polycarbonate plates.

Unfortunately, the process of aging cannot be halted. We are trying to slow it down with as little intervention as possible. The task of conserving and preserving the Dead Sea Scrolls is extremely slow and time-consuming. Although we have been working on it for over ten years now, we still have a long way to go. Since the Dead Sea Scrolls are a universal cultural heritage, it is our duty to safeguard and preserve them for future generations.

Calendars in the Dead Sea Scrolls

James C. VanderKam
John A. O'Brien Professor of Theology
University of Notre Dame

The correct ways of measuring time are an important topic in the Dead Sea Scrolls. More than twenty of the scrolls are calendars of various kinds, and others refer to the subject. It is possible that a dispute over liturgical calendars was one of the factors that led the community of the scrolls to cut themselves off from the Jerusalem temple and their contemporaries, and to pursue an exiled form of life on the shores of the Dead Sea at the place known today as Qumran.

The community associated with the scrolls believed not only that God had created everything but also that he had established specific orders or rules that governed every one and everything in his creation. The sun and moon, the principal markers of time units, operated according to their divinely given laws and never deviated from them. A correct calendar would simply reflect their movements. In addition, God set aside certain times as sacred — the sabbaths and festivals; these had to be celebrated at their correct times or the Lord's will would be violated. The scrolls community believed that their Jewish opponents followed an erroneous calendar, which entailed observing the sacred festivals at non-sacred times, thus mixing the sacred and the profane.

Some history lies behind the calendrical material in the scrolls. The Hebrew Bible or Old Testament says little about times and dates, but in Leviticus 23 and Numbers 28-29 it does legislate exactly when many of the festivals were to take place. A more explicit text is the Astronomical Book of Enoch (1 Enoch 72-82, written perhaps in the third century BCE), which supplies the details for two calendars: a solar year lasting 364 days and a lunar year with 354 days. Several copies of this book were found in Qumran cave 4. The Book of Jubilees (written in about 160-150 BCE), also well represented at Qumran, defends a 364-day solar calendar and describes it as it retells the story of Noah's year-long flood (Genesis 6-8). This author, however, rejects a lunar calendar which, he says, was ten days too short. Both the Astronomical Book and Jubilees are older texts that influenced the Qumran community. We know that the authors of the scrolls accepted a solar year of 364 days from one explicit statement in a text entitled "David's Compositions," part of a very interesting Psalms scroll from cave 11. In it we read that David wrote "364 songs to sing before the altar for the daily perpetual sacrifice, for all the days of the year; and 52 songs for the Sabbath offerings" (11Q5 27:5-7).* Another text, the Temple Scroll, gives a full list of festivals and their dates; in it all information assumes a year of 364 days.

As we turn to the Dead Sea Scrolls that can be called calendars, we should be aware that none of them offers the full range of information that

* Translation of scrolls are slightly modified from Geza Vermes, *The Complete Dead Sea Scrolls in English* (New York and London: Penguin Press, 1997).

we expect in a modern calendar. These texts do allow us to infer many details about a full annual calendar, but the surviving works focus on recording sabbaths and festivals, not every day in a year. A few introductory comments should help us to understand more clearly the information in these texts.

1. In the solar year of 364 days everything is symmetrical. Each of the four three-month periods consists of 91 days (91 × 4 = 364), and in each quarter-year, month 1 has 30 days, month 2 has 30 days, and month 3 has 31 days. Since 364 is exactly divisible by seven, every date falls on the same day of the week every year. Also, the first day of this calendar is a Wednesday, the day on which God created the sun, moon, and stars (Genesis 1:14-19) — the luminaries essential for calendar reckoning. By knowing this one fact, we know on which day of the week every date in the year falls.

Day	months 1,4,7,10	months 2,5,8,11	months 3,6,9,12
Wednesday	1 8 15 22 29	6 13 20 27	4 11 18 25
Thursday	2 9 16 23 30	7 14 21 28	5 12 19 26
Friday	3 10 17 24	1 8 15 22 29	6 13 20 27
Saturday	4 11 18 25	2 9 16 23 30	7 14 21 28
Sunday	5 12 19 26	3 10 17 24	1 8 15 22 29
Monday	6 13 20 27	4 11 18 25	2 9 16 23 30
Tuesday	7 14 21 28	5 12 19 26	3 10 17 24 31

2. The calendrical scrolls make frequent use of a peculiar way of naming the weeks. The priests already in biblical times were divided into twenty-four groups that rotated service at the temple; the reason for the division was probably that there were too many priests for all of them to be serving at the temple at one time. 1 Chronicles 24:7-19 lists all of these divisions by the names of their leaders, and the same chapter traces the division back to the time of David. At some point the practice arose that one of these priestly groups would serve in the temple for one week, at which point it would be relieved by the next one on the list. One unit replaced another on the sabbath, with the first day of its duty being the following day, the first day of the week (Sunday). As a result, one could designate a week by the name of the priestly watch serving in the temple at that time. Each day in the week could be identified by calling it the first day of priestly watch X, the second day of priestly watch X, etc. These are the names of the units:

1. Jehoiarib	7. Hakkoz	13. Huppah	19. Pethahiah
2. Jedaiah	8. Abijah	14. Jeshebeab	20. Jehezkel
3. Harim	9. Jeshua	15. Bilgah	21. Jachin
4. Seorim	10. Shecaniah	16. Immer	22. Gamul
5. Malchijah	11. Eliashib	17. Hezir	23. Delaiah
6. Mijamim	12. Jakim	18. Happizzez	24. Maaziah

These priestly watches also served as a means to define a longer cycle of time. With a total of 24 such units and with 52 full weeks in a year, each would serve for two different seven-day periods each year (2 × 24 = 48) with four weeks left over. As a result the first four groups would serve a third week in the first year, the second four groups would do so in the second year, etc. After six years, each of the 24 watches would have served an extra third week (6 × 4 = 24), which would mean that after six years the first watch would again be serving in the first week of the year. In this way, the sequence of priestly watches came to define a six-year period.

The idea that the priestly watches who preside over the earthly worship of God in the temple operate in tandem with the celestial luminaries says something about the harmony these people saw in God's universe.

Turning to the calendar texts themselves, we can divide them into a few types.

1. Lists of sabbaths and festivals

A simple example is 4Q327 (4QCalendrical Document D), which enumerates the dates on which sabbaths and festivals fall. A section of the text reads:

On the sixteenth (day) in (the fifth month) is
    a sabbath.
On the twenty-third (day) in (the fifth month) is
    a sabbath.
[On the th]irtieth [in (the fifth month) is
    a sabbath]...
[On the twenty-firs]t (day) in (the sixth month) is
    a sabbath.
On the twenty-second (day) in (the sixth month)
    is the festival of oil.
Af[ter the sab]bath ... is the Offeri[ng of wood].

If we consult our chart of the completely schematic solar calendar, a sabbath can fall on the sixteenth only in months 2, 5, 8, and 11. The short text does not indicate which of these months is involved, but from other information in the scrolls we know that a festival of oil occurred in the sixth month, the twenty-second day. Hence we can conclude that this part of the text gives us dates in months five and six.

2. Lists of dates for sabbaths and festivals using priestly watches

4Q320 (4QCalendrical Document A) frg. 4 iii 1-10:

The first year: its feasts. On the third (day in the week of) Maaziah: the Passover.

On the 1st (day) [in (the week of) Jeda[iah]: the Waving of the [Sheaf].

On the 5th (day) in (the week of) Seorim: the [Second] Passover. *Vacat*

On the 1st (day) in (the week of) Jeshua: the Feast of Weeks.

On the 4th (day) in (the week of) Maaziah: the Day of Memorial.

[On] the 6th (day) in Jehoiarib: the Day of Atonement [in the] seventh [month]. *Vacat*

[On the 4th (day) in (the week of) Jeda]iah: the Feast of Tabernacles.

The second (year): its feasts ...

With the list of priestly watches from 1 Chronicles 24 in front of us, we can easily calculate the dates for all of the festivals listed. Many of these are also stated in the Bible and are thus not in doubt; in other cases, however, where the Bible does not specify festival dates, we have early evidence in the scrolls for when this particular community celebrated them. Maaziah is the last of the twenty-four groups in the list in 1 Chronicles. If Passover, which the Bible dates to 1/14, occurred on the third day of Maaziah's week of service, this group must have begun serving on 1/12. Hence its seven-day term of duty ran from 1/12 to 1/18.

The next festival — Waving of the Sheaf — is an especially interesting one because it was at the center of an ancient Jewish calendrical controversy. This waving ceremony took place after Passover and was the beginning point for the fifty-day count to the Festival of Weeks, but the Bible dates neither the ceremony nor the Festival of Weeks. Leviticus says only that the sheaf ceremony was to take place on the day after the sabbath (Leviticus 23:9-16). The word "sabbath" is potentially ambiguous; besides its literal meaning, it can signify "holiday" in biblical usage. Thus, some ancient Jewish scholars understood the Leviticus text to mean that the date in question was the day after a holiday, while others took it to mean a Sunday.

Our passage from 4QCalendrical Document A allows us to figure out what the scrolls community thought about this problem. The Waving of the Sheaf takes place on the first day of Jedaiah, the second name in the list of watches. If Maaziah, the last name, served from 1/12-18, then Jehoiarib, the first name in the list of 1 Chronicles 24, served from 1/19-25. As a result, the first day of Jedaiah would have been 1/26 — the first Sunday after the festival sequence of Passover-Unleavened Bread (1/14-21). So, the group understood "the day after the sabbath" to be a literal Sunday after the last festival to be mentioned in Leviticus's list of holidays.

Our text also tells us when the Festival of Weeks

(fifty days after the sheaf ceremony) occurred: the first day in Jeshua's week. Jeshua is the ninth name in 1 Chronicles 24, and if we place the third-eighth priestly groups before it and assume the 364-day calendar, the first day of Jeshua's service is 3/15 — the date for the Festival of Weeks implied in the Book of Jubilees. This was apparently not the time when the festival was celebrated by other Jewish groups.

3. Coordinating dates in solar and lunar calendars

A more complicated kind of listing coordinates festivals and sabbaths with the priestly watches *and* with lunar dates. A few lines from 4Q321 (4QCalendrical Document B) will illustrate the type (4Q321 2 ii 7-8):

> [On the fifth (day) in (the week of) Harim] which is on the twelfth (day) of the twelfth month. And the New Moo[n] is on the sabbath [in (the week of)] Mijamin which is on the twenty-eighth (day) in (the twelfth month).

The text not only refers to two calendrical systems (the dates are in a solar calendar, the new moon is obviously part of a lunar calculation) but also coordinates two events in a lunar cycle — some-thing that occurred on the 12th of the month in question and something that happened on the 28th of the month. The translation given above assumes that the latter is the new moon, but there is some dispute about the meaning of the term, with some scholars preferring to relate it to the full moon. At any rate, the text is giving the dates for both the new and full moon in terms of their corresponding dates in the solar calendar.

The Qumran caves have yielded other kinds of calendrical texts, even ones that serve divinatory purposes, but the ones surveyed above give a cross-section of the kinds of data available in the Dead Sea Scrolls. The calendars can be monotonous to read, but they relate to larger issues. As noted earlier, the group followed a different system for reckoning time than their fellow Jews did, and thus distanced them-selves from their co-religionists in a practical way.

The calendars of Qumran raise a practical problem. The actual solar year is not 364 but 365.25 days. Also, the Jewish calendar must agree with the solar year because several of the festivals are tied to particular harvest seasons. Hence it is likely that the group developed a method of intercalation to bring their system into harmony with the true solar year, but we do not know for sure how they did this. It is likely, however, that at some intervals they would have added complete seven-day units to maintain the harmony of the system.

Abegg • Alexander • Allegro • Anderson • Attridge • Baillet
Baker • Barthélemy • Baumgarten • Ben-Dov • Benoit
Bernstein • Brady • Brooke • Broshi • Charlesworth • Chazon
Cohen • Collins • Cotton • Cross • E. Crowfoot • G. Crowfoot
Davila • de Vaux • Dimant • Duncan • Elgvin • Ernst • E. Eshel
H. Eshel • Falk • Fitzmyer • Flint • Fuller • García Martínez
Glessmer • Greenfield • Grohmann • Gropp • Harrington
Herbert • Jastram • Kister • Kraft • Lange • Larson • Lehman
Leith • Lemaire • Lim • Metso • Milik • Misgav • Mittmann-
Richert • Morgenstern • Murphy • Naveh • Newsom • Niccum
Nitzan • Olyan • Parry • Pfann • Pike • Puech • Qimron
Sanders • Sanderson • Schiffman • Schuller • Seely • Segal
Skehan • Skinner • Smith • Sokoloff • Starcky • Stegemann
Steudel • Stone • Strugnell • Stuckenbruck • Sussmann
Szink • Talmon • Tanzer • Tigchelaar • Tov • Trebolle Barrera
Ulrich • VanderKam • Vermes • Weinfeld • White Crawford
van der Woude • Yardeni • Zissu

Celebrating the Completion of the Publication of the Dead Sea Scrolls*

Emanuel Tov
Professor of Bible
Hebrew University, Jerusalem
Editor-in-Chief
Discoveries in the Judaean Desert

In November of 2001, I was pleased to be able to announce that the publication of all the Dead Sea Scrolls was completed within the official series, *Discoveries in the Judaean Desert (DJD),* and its smaller sister operations, the Masada series, the Judean Desert Series, and a few individual volumes. I am happy to inform the public that all the scrolls, or rather, all the fragments from the Judean Desert have now been presented to the scholarly world in the form of critical editions, mainly in the *DJD,* but also in earlier and subsequent publications. After 54 years of excitement, expectation, tribulation, much criticism and a little praise, with the help of much inspiration, and even more perspiration, the publication has been finalized.

The publication process of the Qumran scrolls has taken some time, possibly a little too long but, in actual fact, not overly long for 37 volumes together with all the inventories and supporting publications. The publication of the scrolls has been completed due to the work and devotion, over the course of five decades, of 98 text editors,[1] several volume editors and consulting editors, aided and assisted by the production teams in Jerusalem and at the University of Notre Dame. I write this essay as the one who has organized and guided the editorial work over the past decade. We are all in debt to the Israel Antiquities Authority, Oxford Univeristy Press (OUP), publisher of the *DJD* series, the Oxford Centre for Postgraduate Hebrew Studies, the Dead Sea Scrolls Foundation, and of course, to the goat.

The preparations for each individual volume were lengthy. They did not have to take several decades, but nevertheless the process is time-consuming. Had the initial team in the 1950s consisted of twenty, thirty, or even fifty scholars, and not just of nine, the publication *could* have been completed some time ago. If more funds had been available from the beginning, greater progress could have been made, but I don't think that insufficient financial support was the major reason for the delay. The limited size of the initial team, lack of organization of the publication procedure, a lack of experience, and certain prejudices were probably the main contributing factors for early delays. Even if Father Roland de Vaux would have had ample funds, computers, and e-mail, the volumes would not have gone to press quickly, since the organization lacked the necessary insights.

All the same, the latest generation of scholars would not have succeeded in our task without the valuable input of our predecessors. We still

* The original text of this address was delivered at a festive session chaired by J. A. Sanders at the annual meeting of the Society of Biblical Literature on November 15, 2001. Some notes have been added in the written version.

1. The facing page lists the names of these editors.

stand on the shoulders of that first generation of scholars who did all the preparatory groundwork upon which all our own efforts are based. We have all benefited immeasurably from the work of John Strugnell, Józéf Milik, Frank Moore Cross, Jr., Eliezer Lippa Sukenik, Yigael Yadin, Jacob Licht, David Flusser, and Shemaryahu Talmon, just to name a few. Without these and many other masters, we would not be where we are today in scholarship and in the publication process. Some of them pieced the fragments together and had them photographed in a masterly fashion. And it was they who devised the *DJD* system and began the research.

Yes, it took a while, but as my predecessor, John Strugnell, used to remind us, the preparation of the *DJD* series did not take as long as the publication of similar corpora. The greater part of the Cairo Genizah fragments is still awaiting redemption after more than a century. By the same token, the Greek Oxyrhynchus papyri are far from being published after one century. The British Academy has recently voted to support this enterprise for a second century: yes, a second *century*. Strugnell made the point that the publication of one volume in the papyrus collections of Rylands, Berlin, Tebtunis, Michigan, and Oxyrhynchus took an average of 7.2 years.[2]

Other large projects moved ahead more quickly, but the half century taken for the publication of the voluminous amount of material from the various sites in the Judean Desert is not excessive. Beyond our original assignment, we also published material found in 1986 and 1993 at Jericho (vol. XXXVIII) and some fragments that surfaced only in recent years, as well as the seal impressions and texts from Wadi Daliyeh, beyond the Judean Desert (vol. XXIV). I therefore suggest that we now remove from our vocabulary the words which have so often been voiced following Geza Vermes's first use of them in 1977, namely that the "greatest . . . of all Hebrew . . . manuscript discoveries is likely to become the academic scandal *par excellence* of the twentieth century."[3] Vermes only said that this project was *likely* to become a scandal. Well, it hasn't. The publication of the more than 1500 texts from the Judean Desert, 900 of which were derived from Qumran, within half a century is appropriate for a corpus of this magnitude.

The academic world and the public eagerly awaited the Dead Sea Scrolls editions and, as promised, they were published, mainly over the past decade, in 28 volumes and a concordance, with

2. See J. Strugnell, 'The Original Team of Editors', in *On Scrolls, Artefacts and Intellectual Property* (ed. T. H. Lim et al.; JSPSup 38; Sheffield: Sheffield Academic Press, 2001) 178–92 (189).

3. See G. Vermes, 'Access to the Dead Sea Scrolls; Fifty Years of Personal Experience', in *On Scrolls, Artefacts and Intellectual Property*, 193–8 (193).

two more in preparation. Our 28 volumes compare well with the eight volumes produced by the earlier editorial team over the previous four decades.

In order that there be no misunderstanding, let me clarify what it means to say that the publication of all the Dead Sea Scrolls has been completed. What has the publication project achieved to date? All the Qumran fragments have been made available in critical editions and photographic form, mainly in the official *DJD* series. Several re-editions have also been published in a series edited by James Charlesworth.[4]

In 1990, we were thinking in terms of the *DJD* series containing 30 volumes, but a decade later we have ended up with 37 large-sized volumes. Of these volumes, 24 are devoted solely to cave 4, just a little more than the four volumes envisaged by Lankester Harding in 1955 for the series as a whole![5] In fact, to date, 35 volumes have rolled off the press, in 2001 alone five volumes. Vol. XXXIX, the introduction to the series, has been published in 2002. This introductory volume of 452 pages contains a host of lists and information about the *DJD* texts and editions. The Samuel volume will be sent to the press shortly. That brings the series to a current total of 37 volumes or 11,984 pages and 1,348 plates (including vol XVII). The last volume of Aramaic texts[6] and a few re-editions are being prepared by the Notre Dame team in stage 2 of the project,[7] which will bring the final number of volumes in the series to 41 or 42.

We do not only celebrate the publication of the *DJD*, however; we also commemorate the completion of *all* the Dead Sea Scrolls, which involves much more than *DJD*. It so happens that in 2001 we have seen the release of the third and last volume in the Judaean Desert Series, recording the texts from Israeli excavations in Naḥal Ḥever.[8] It is a complicated matter to keep track of who

4. J. H. Charlesworth (ed.), *The Dead Sea Scrolls, Hebrew, Aramaic, and Greek Texts with English Translations,* vols. 1–3, 4A–4B, 6B (Tübingen/Louisville: Mohr/Westminster John Knox, 1994, 1995, 1996, 1997, 1999, 2001).

5. When trying to locate a press willing to publish the scrolls, G. Lankester Harding wrote that he was thinking in terms of 'altogether, perhaps, five volumes.' The letter is archived in Folder 1118 of the Palestine Archaeological Museum.

6. E. Puech, *Qumran Cave 4.XXVII: Textes araméens, deuxi me partie: 4Q550–575* (DJD XXXVII; Oxford: Clarendon).

7. M. Bernstein and G. Brooke with the assistance of J. Høgenhavn, in consultation with J. VanderKam and M. Brady, *Qumran Cave 4.I: 4Q158–186* (DJD Va; Revised edition; Oxford: Clarendon); P. W. Flint and E. Ulrich, *Qumran Cave 1.II: The Isaiah Scrolls* (DJD XXXII; Oxford: Clarendon).

8. Y. Yadin, J. C. Greenfield, A. Yardeni, and B. A. Levine, *The Documents from the Bar Kochba Period in the Cave of Letters: Hebrew, Aramaic and Nabatean-Aramaic Papyri* (JDS 3; Jerusalem: IES, Institute of Archaeology, Hebrew University, Shrine of the Book, Israel Museum, 2002).

excavated what, and because of this, some Naḥal
Ḥever texts have been published in *DJD* XXVII
and XXXVIII, and others elsewhere. With the publication of this third volume, for which we are *not*
responsible, we are pleased to announce that all
the Dead Sea Scrolls beyond *DJD* have also been
published, namely in the Judaean Desert Series
(3 volumes),[9] the Masada series (3 volumes),[10] and
several volumes elsewhere, such as the Temple
Scroll, and the editions from cave 1 in the 1950s.[11]
Altogether, we are talking about 15 such volumes.

Therefore, if you still follow my arithmetic, the
publication of this essay celebrates 37 *DJD* vol-

umes and 15 volumes beyond *DJD*. The fragments
from the Judean Desert are therefore available in
52 large volumes. As previously mentioned, a few
re-editions are still expected from Notre Dame and
Trinity Western University.

Texts are necessarily accompanied by concordances. The official concordances for all the texts
from the Judean Desert, not only Qumran, are now
being prepared by M. Abegg, with J.E. Bowley
and E.M. Cook. The first volume containing the
nonbiblical texts from Qumran is being released
now.[12] Abegg also made all the nonbiblical Dead
Sea Scrolls available electronically within the
Accordance computer program which enables very
sophisticated searches and the making of concordances for individual scrolls. This program oper-
ates on the Macintosh, but this program can now
also be used on the PC with an emulation program.

The first three parts of the Comprehensive Edition
of the Dead Sea Scrolls arranged by subject (D.W.
Parry, E. Tov) are being released now.[13] Gene Ulrich
is planning a similar volume for the biblical texts.

When all is said and done, in a little more than
a decade, we will have produced thirty volumes:

9. See the previous note and further: Y. Yadin, *The Finds from the
Bar Kochba Period in the Cave of the Letters* (JDS 1; Jerusalem: IES,
1963); N. Lewis, *The Documents from the Bar-Kochba Period in the
Cave of Letters—Greek Papyri* (JDS 2; Jerusalem, IES, Institute of
Archaeology, Hebrew University, Shrine of the Book, Israel Museum,
1989).

10. Y. Yadin and J. Naveh, *Masada I. The Aramaic and Hebrew
Ostraca and Jar Inscriptions* (Jerusalem: IES and Hebrew University
of Jerusalem, 1989); H. M. Cotton and J. Geiger, *Masada II, The Yigal
Yadin Excavations 1963–1965, Final Reports: The Latin and Greek
Documents* (Jerusalem: IES, 1989); S. Talmon and Y. Yadin, *Masada VI,
The Yigal Yadin Excavations 1963–1965, Final Reports* (Jerusalem: IES
and Hebrew University of Jerusalem, 1999).

11. I refer mainly to the large texts from cave 1 (that is, the Isaiah
scrolls, the Thanksgiving Scroll, etc.) and cave 11 (the main copy of
the Temple Scroll and the paleo-Hebrew Leviticus scroll), as well as
A. Grohmann, *Arabic Papyri from Hirbet el-Mird* (Bibliothèque du
Muséon 52; Louvain, 1963); J. T. Milik, *The Books of Enoch* (Oxford:
Clarendon, 1976).

12. M. G. Abegg, Jr., with J.E. Bowley and E.M. Cook in consultation
with E. Tov, *The Dead Sea Scrolls Concordance, Volume One: The Non-
biblical Texts from Qumran* (Leiden: E. J. Brill, 2003).

13. D.W. Parry and E. Tov, *The Dead Sea Scrolls: A Comprehensive
Edition Arranged by Subject* (Leiden: E.J. Brill, 2003).

six at Notre Dame, a Concordance at Trinity Western; and twenty-three volumes in Jerusalem. Not included in this figure are the three volumes of supplements and re-editions to be produced at Notre Dame and Trinity Western within the next two years.

I also suggest that we remove from our vocabulary the term 'the liberation of the scrolls' by which was meant the 'liberation of the photographs.' After all, many photographs of the fragments have been available for many years in the various text editions published since 1950. In 1991 a facsimile edition of all the positives was published; an edition whose source is shrouded in everlasting mystery.[14] A microfiche edition of all the images was published in 1993,[15] and a good CD of all the photographs was published by Brill in 1997 and 1999.[16] As far as I can tell, however, none of these tools was used much.

14. R. H. Eisenman and J. M. Robinson, *A Facsimile Edition of the Dead Sea Scrolls* (Washington, D.C.: Biblical Archaeology Society, 1991).

15. E. Tov with the collaboration of S. J. Pfann: *The Dead Sea Scrolls on Microfiche—A Comprehensive Facsimile Edition of the Texts from the Judean Desert, with a Companion Volume* (Leiden: E. J. Brill and IDC, 1993, 1995).

16. T. Lim in consultation with P. Alexander, *The Dead Sea Scrolls— Electronic Reference Library* (Oxford/Leiden: Oxford University Press and E. J. Brill, 1997). For the 1999 release, see note n. 17.

The scrolls were not incarcerated, and therefore did not need to be liberated. There were definitely no liberators or scholars receiving the so-called liberated photographs with open arms. The real incarceration of the scrolls was their imprisonment in photographs available to all from 1991, and their virtual neglect was due to the users' inability to read them. The real liberation of the scrolls took place with their inclusion in scholarly editions available to all.

Because of the availability of all these sources, it cannot really be said that the scrolls have been concealed or were inaccessible during the 1990s, as has been asserted innumerable times. However, the public at large thought and possibly still thinks that they are largely inaccessible, because that's what journalists have led them to believe. Unfortunately, also for most scholars many scrolls appeared not to exist, so to speak, since they did not consult the tools containing the *photographs* of the scrolls. Indeed, this situation reveals a paradoxical aspect of the criticism voiced against the international team over the last two decades. When all the images were finally made available in 1991, following a major public outcry for the publication of the scrolls, they were hardly used. These photographs remained *terra incognita* for most scholars, since even specialists in the field need a very skilled eye in order to use them. It is

also nearly impossible to find one's way through
the veritable labyrinth of photographs prepared
mainly in the 1950s if one is looking for a specific
Qumran text. After all, most compositions are
comprised of many fragments scattered among a
number of these photographs. A combination of
the dispersal of the fragments and the technical
difficulties in reading the photographs therefore
made the use of the available photographs almost
a Mission Impossible. However, today we have at
our disposal the Brill CD of the texts prepared by
the Foundation for Ancient Research and Mormon
Studies (FARMS) at Brigham Young University,
the second version of which was released in 1999,
containing almost all Qumran texts and images,
together with a reasonable search program.[17]

What the general public as well as many
scholars have been more interested in, however,
are translations of the scrolls. These have been
rolling from many presses in many languages
since the 1950s. One can now follow the words of
the Teacher Who is Right (The Righteous Teacher)
not only in the major European languages, but
also in Yiddish, Spanish, Portuguese, Dutch, Ital-
ian, Hungarian, Polish, Danish, Russian, Japanese,

and Finnish.[18] However, all these translations are
incomplete or imperfect, having been prepared
before the completion of the research for the
official publication of the fragments. It takes years
for a scholar to disentangle the web of relations
between tiny fragments of a certain composition,
rendering it simply inconceivable that the translations published so far present these fragments
correctly. Therefore, now that the first round of
research has been completed and is available in the
DJD series, a second round of translations can be
embarked upon.

The public has awaited scholars who are masters
not only of all the technical skills of the publication process, but are also familiar with the literary
genre of each composition. The publication of any
text is a work of love and selfless dedication, of
trial and error, of excitement but often also of
despair, and at the end, of seeing the light. I'm not

17. E. Tov (ed.), *The Dead Sea Scrolls Database (Non-Biblical Texts)* (The Dead Sea Scrolls Electronic Reference Library, Vol. 2; Prepared by the Foundation for Ancient Research and Mormon Studies [FARMS]) (Leiden: E. J. Brill, 1999).

18. For some bibliographical references, see: S. Glassman, *Megiles fun Yam Hamelach* (New York: Knight Publishing Corp., 1965); F. García Martínez, *Textos de Qumrán* (Madrid: Trotta, 1992); id., *Textos de Qumran. Edição fiel e completa dos Documentos do Mar Morto* (Petrópolis: Vozes, 1995); id., and A. S. van der Woude, *De rollen van de Dode Zee* 1-2 (Kampen/Tielt: Kok/Lannoo, 1994–95); id., *Testi de Qumran (Biblica 4), Edizione italiana a cura di C. Martone* (Brescia: Paideia, 1996); P. Muchowski, *Rekopisy znad morza martwego Qumran–Wadi Murabba'at–Masada* (Biblioteka zwojów tlo Nowego Testamentu 5; Cracow: Enigma Press, 1996); R. Sollamo, *Qumranin Kirjasto* (Helsinki: University Press, 1997); B. Ejrnaes et al., *Dødehavs Skrifterne* (Frederiksberg: ANIS, 1998).

referring to the light seen at the end of the tunnel when one is approaching the end of a project, but rather that stage in the preparation of a text when you finally understand the fragments as part of a whole. We continuously struggle with such questions as the identification of the fragments, their sequence, the number of manuscripts of a given composition and the relation between them. Then, all of a sudden, in a flash of enlightenment you are able to make sense of it all and you understand what you have been working on for years. That is a moment of immense satisfaction. I have seen how scholars suddenly receive a flash of enlightenment. Of course, I should add, mild pressure from an editor-in-chief often aids a scholar in reaching that moment of truth.

The larger picture consists of many details, the decipherment of the individual letters, the connection between the fragments, and above all the reconstruction of the *missing* letters and words. O, those *lacunae*, so often the backbone and justification of our scholarly work, that add so much *spice* to our lives! These reconstructions make the production of an edition a veritable work of art. A very subjective creation, as all works of art, and not a product whose correctness can be proven. There is no right or wrong in this area for the simple reason that every scholar who sets out to produce an edition will reach different conclusions. Since the composition that the scholar sets out to reconstruct remains hypothetical, even in the case of a biblical manuscript, it usually cannot be proven whether a specific reconstruction is correct or not. I once heard a law professor lecturing on the copyright issue relating to the Dead Sea Scrolls. That professor compared the possible copyright of reconstructions of scrolls to the alphabetical listing of the American citizens and 'the work of a potter who glued together the pieces of a broken ancient vase.'[19] However, in the latter two cases, there is only one right solution, while in case of the scrolls there is an endless number of solutions, each one the brainchild of an individual scholar, and all equally possible.

The production process of these text editions was long and complicated.[20] My planning in 1990 pertained to the following issues: (1) preparation of camera-ready editions and plates; (2) arrangements to be made with OUP; (3) fund-raising; (4) the expansion of the team of scholars to a size which would enable the completion of the project.

19. This paper has now appeared in print. See C. A. Carson, 'The Application of American Copyright Law to the Dead Sea Scrolls Controversy,' in *On Scrolls, Artefacts and Intellectual Property*, 74–98 (79, 81).

20. For details, see my description "The *Discoveries in the Judaean Desert* Series: History and System of Presentation," in *The Texts from the Judaean Desert: Indices and an Introduction to the* Discoveries in the Judaean Desert *Series* (ed. E. Tov, DJD XXXIX; Oxford: Clarendon, 2002) 1–25.

In any event, by the time I became editor-in-chief, the fragments had been cleaned, sorted, photographed, as well as identified and partially inventoried. The claim has often been made that this important work was completed in the mid-1950s, but the identification, photographing, and inventorying continued to take much of our time and energy. Initial identifications and the grouping of fragments turned out to be very helpful, but opinions changed and regrouping and re-identification became necessary. When a group of fragments that was once considered to represent a single Qumran composition was identified as representing two separate compositions, a new Qumran scroll was born, so to speak, creating a new entry in our list. In this way, the number of Qumran scrolls, once complete, has grown in our imagination from 600 to 900, together with several hundred documents from the other sites in the Judean Desert.

We also had to give names to the compositions. The story of the name-giving warrants a novel in its own right. Once included in the official edition, a name can no longer be changed. Some of these names are utterly subjective; for example, we are still haunted by the so-called 'Wiles of the Wicked Woman' (4Q184), so named by John Allegro. According to many, even the name 'Temple Scroll' is a misnomer, and with apologies to James Sanders, 11QPsalms[a] may *not* be a biblical scroll.

John Strugnell believed that *Musar le-mevin* (according to his vocalization, not *la-mevin*) was the original name of 4Q416–423 in antiquity, and as I could not convince him otherwise, I suggested 4QInstruction as a counterproposal. Neither of us could be convinced, and therefore the name on the title page of vol. XXXIV is a compromise: 4QInstruction (*4QMusar le-mevin*).

Cataloguing has also been a major part of our work. When we began in 1991, we found only partial lists of the compositions, assignments to scholars, photographs, holdings in the Rockefeller Museum building, and most importantly, the correlation between these lists. Helpful lists by Steve Reed of the Ancient Biblical Manuscript Center (ABMC) in Claremont, California, were in the making.[21] At that point, together with Steve Pfann, I set out to compile a comprehensive database, and that tool, the final form of which was published in the introduction volume (vol. XXXIX) served as the central reference apparatus of the project. In it we recorded the text names together with their various identifying numbers and the names of the scholars assigned to edit each text, along with the bibliographical information concerning preliminary and final publications.

21. S. A. Reed and M. J. Lundberg, *The Dead Sea Scrolls Catalogue — Documents, Photographs and Museum Inventory Numbers* (SBLRBS 32; Atlanta, Georgia 1994).

I was involved also in Carbon-14 examinations of some twenty documents.[22] The choice of the manuscripts and the sampling of the few square millimetres of the documents was a painstaking and instructive process. I will never forget the tears in the eyes of Lena Libman, the conservator at the Rockefeller Museum, when she had to cut out a few square millimetres of surface for these Carbon-14 tests. But the sacrifice of precious parchment paid off when the Carbon-14 tests basically corroborated the paleographic dating of the scrolls assigned by Frank Moore Cross and other scholars.

It became clear to me that the only chance of completing the publication was to prepare the camera-ready pages ourselves, since alternative procedures were extremely cumbersome. Gene Ulrich was more knowledgeable than I in the computer-assisted preparation of editions, so I decided to adapt and improve for the whole team whatever system he was using. We therefore opted for the use of Macintosh computers, and typed Hebrew backwards in MS Word. It worked so beautifully that even with the passing of years, I decided not to employ more advanced programs; if it works, it works. For the coordination of an international project, a step forward is often a step backwards.

Our standardization allowed the editors to submit their work electronically, and, indeed, during the last years of the project almost every editor prepared the first drafts on his or her own Mac. However, some preferred PCs, and one scholar continued to submit hand-written editions until the very end.

According to my master plan, twenty-three non-biblical volumes would be prepared in Jerusalem, and one non-biblical and five biblical volumes at Notre Dame. Funding arrived annually from the Oxford Centre for Postgraduate Studies, for which we were very grateful, but this funding was insufficient for the activities I had in mind. Dr. Weston Fields and I therefore created The Dead Sea Scrolls Foundation, now headed by Shalom Paul, which together with the Oxford allowance supported our work.[23] In addition, Gene Ulrich and Jim VanderKam of Notre Dame were well supported by funds from the National Endowment for the Humanities.

The re-organization of the team and re-assignment of the texts created delicate problems. In practical terms, it implied that texts had to be

---

22. A. J. T. Jull, D. J. Donahue, M. Broshi, and E. Tov, "Radiocarbon Dating of Scrolls and Linen Fragments from the Judean Desert," *Radiocarbon* 37 (1995) 11–19.

23. We needed support for a secretary and typists/copy-editors who would format or reformat the texts and prepare the camera-ready manuscripts and plates. Further support was required for scholars who needed assistants at their home universities, while a few also received funding enabling them to examine their scrolls in Jerusalem.

taken from scholars to whom so many items had been assigned that, in order to complete their work, their lifespans would have to compete with that of Methuselah. It was a very unpleasant task and resulted, for example, in J.T. Milik ceasing to cooperate with us.

With the involvement of the Israel Antiquities Authority and the enthusiastic support of its former director, Amir Drori, the publication enterprise was reorganized and enlarged from 1990 onwards under my own direction, and new appointments were made periodically until the very end of the publication project. By 1990, nineteen scholars had completed their assignments and twenty-six of the earlier editors remained on the team.[24] With the appointment of fifty-three new scholars, the overall number of editors who worked on the project totaled ninety-eight.

Who were these 98 *DJD* editors[25] and from which disciplines did they come? Some of them focused almost exclusively on the texts from the Judean Desert. But since there is no clearly defined disci-pline of Scrolls research, most scholars came from a variety of backgrounds, focusing on either the textual criticism or exegesis of Hebrew Scripture, intertestamental literature, Apocrypha, Septuagint, New Testament, or philology in general. When choosing editors, the only criterion used was that of proven competence. This implied an increase in the percentage of Israeli scholars who had been barred from this work during the first decades of the publication. Over the past decade, the members of the international team have consisted equally of scholars from North America, Europe, and Israel; the cooperation between these scholars has usually been superb.

How did we work? Beyond the preparatory activities for the publication and organization of the team, the editor-in-chief organized the assignments, provided scholars with photographs, and guided his colleagues as much as he could. I was in touch with all the editors on a consistent basis. That is why, at the peak of our activities, I met with 20–30 colleagues at the annual gatherings of

24. The size of the first international team has never been clear, neither to its members nor to the outside world. Of this group, eight continued to be actively engaged in producing editions during J. Strugnell's term as editor-in-chief, during which time eighteen new members were appointed, adding up to a total of twenty-six actively involved scholars.

25. The scholars who were involved in the publication of the Dead Sea Scrolls were usually called 'editors' since they produced critical editions of these scrolls, either in *DJD* or elsewhere. This term is somewhat misleading, since an 'editor' is also someone who edits the work of others. Therefore, within the *DJD* editions, these scholars were considered 'authors,' whose work was usually edited by a volume editor or a consulting editor.

the Society of Biblical Literature. Everyone realized that our production office was eagerly awaiting his or her manuscript. In fact, it is actually a marvel, with so many volumes having been published over the years, that our work was always well spread out. There was hardly ever an overabundance or lack of work at the production offices.

More than other scholars, editors of editions work in isolation, without much feedback, and they therefore needed the interaction with us. Rather than waiting for the completed manuscripts, I therefore asked for parts, enabling the production staff to make progress on the edition, and thus providing the editor with the necessary interaction. We often aided editors in organizing their thoughts, both before they submitted their manuscripts and afterwards. Many a mistake was thus prevented at the eleventh hour by a member of our staff, even at the preparation stage of the concordances of the individual volumes.

Modern technology has been very meaningful for the project and the completion of 29 volumes in twelve years was not only due to our organization, editors, production staffs, and financial support. The *DJD* series would not be where it is today without our computers, laser printers, scanners, and e-mail. I bless the day I made the decision to prepare the camera-ready copy myself. This decision created much headache and it turned

us into a printing press, but without this procedure little would have been accomplished. The first four volumes were prepared in Jerusalem on a little Macintosh SE without a hard drive. However, over the last few years, *DJD* editions have been submitted to our advanced Macintosh computers by e-mail and no longer on diskettes or, as earlier, on paper. The files of the last volume, that of Samuel, must have traversed cyber-space hundreds of times with all their color-codes denoting different types of changes.

Some volumes were easier to prepare than others, but one thing is clear: by definition, there *is* no easy *DJD* volume. I don't know whether a one- or two-author volume was easier than a volume authored by thirty authors, such as vol. XXXVI. The personalities of the authors were the determining factor rather than the nature of the texts. Furthermore, the English of some editions required major rewriting. Some scholars were either too concise or too verbose. Some derogatory remarks made by editors about their colleagues needed to be toned down or removed altogether. Some scholars prepared their own plates, while we prepared them for others.

We succeeded in most missions, but definitely not in all, mainly due to a lack of the necessary cooperation. I wanted to include re-editions of the Genesis Apocryphon and more Enoch texts in the series, but was not successful. I almost struck a deal with regard to the Greek fragments from Khirbet Mird found in Belgium, but at the last moment the deal fell through. These fragments now continue to be moved back and forth at ten-yearly intervals between the Universities who exercise joint custodianship, the Flemish University of Leuven and the French University of Louvain. And although archaeological artifacts were not part of our assignment, we tried to push for the publication of archaeological data, but without success, not even with regard to the inscribed Qumran jar handles, which, as far as I know, are housed either in the École Biblique or in Paris.

Of course, I had no idea what I had agreed to at an IAA meeting in August 1990, when I was pressured to accept the editorship. I doubt whether I would have ever agreed to this assignment had I realized the enormity of the enterprise, the struggles with several establishments, and the daily pressures involved in convincing editors to finish their texts. One such time when I definitely regretted having accepted this challenge was in 1991 when all hell broke out, with major attacks being made on our team, while I was still inexperienced. At that time Jim Sanders and Frank Cross called me on the phone informing me of the imminent release of photographs by The Huntington Library, a library which was, at the time, totally unfamiliar to me.

DJD is a series which contains first editions, *editiones principes*, the plural of *editio princeps*. This essay celebrates the end product of the publication project, which at the same time marks the beginning of a process of exegesis, and of the defining and redefining of the nature of the compositions.

To all the institutions and individuals mentioned in this essay, and many more, I owe a great debt and, of course, also to the goat. In his preface to *The Ancient Library of Qumran*, Frank Moore Cross thanked his patient wife, Betty Anne, 'who wishes, I am sure, that the scrolls had been fed to the goat responsible for their discovery.' Obviously, this goat did not eat all the Cave 1 scrolls. But lately I have developed a new theory in which I contend that this clever goat was a selective glutton; he only ate the scrolls that would have been damaging to Christianity and Judaism.

About this Catalog

This catalog is divided into two main sections. The first, "From the Qumran Caves," describes the 12 scroll fragments included in the exhibition. The second section, "From the Qumran Ruin," presents artifacts excavated at the nearby Qumran ruin in addition to scroll jars from the caves.

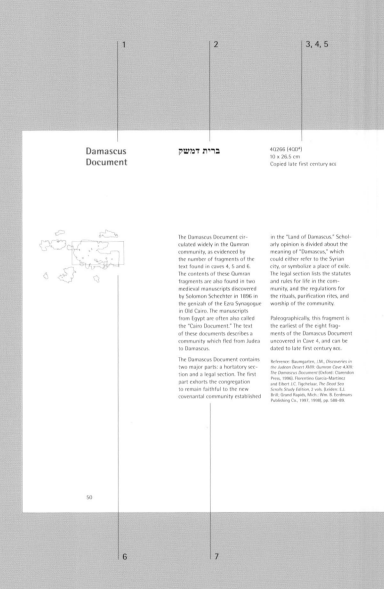

1   2   3, 4, 5

Damascus Document

ברית דמשק

4Q266 (4QD^a)
10 x 26.5 cm
Copied late first century BCE

The Damascus Document circulated widely in the Qumran community, as evidenced by the number of fragments of the text found in caves 4, 5 and 6. The contents of these Qumran fragments are also found in two medieval manuscripts discovered by Solomon Schechter in 1896 in the genizah of the Ezra Synagogue in Old Cairo. The manuscripts from Egypt are often also called the "Cairo Document." The text of these documents describes a community which fled from Judea to Damascus.

The Damascus Document contains two major parts: a hortatory section and a legal section. The first part exhorts the congregation to remain faithful to the new covenantal community established

in the "Land of Damascus." Scholarly opinion is divided about the meaning of "Damascus," which could either refer to the Syrian city, or symbolize a place of exile. The legal section lists the statutes and rules for life in the community, and the regulations for the rituals, purification rites, and worship of the community.

Paleographically, this fragment is the earliest of the eight fragments of the Damascus Document uncovered in Cave 4, and can be dated to late first century BCE.

Reference: Baumgarten, J.M., *Discoveries in the Judean Desert XVIII: Qumran Cave 4.XIII: The Damascus Document* (Oxford: Clarendon Press, 1996). Florentino García-Martínez and Eibert J.C. Tigchelaar, *The Dead Sea Scrolls Study Edition*, 2 vols. (Leiden: E.J. Brill; Grand Rapids, Mich.: Wm. B. Eerdmans Publishing Co., 1997, 1998), pp. 588-89.

50

6   7

The curatorial descriptions of the scrolls include the following elements:

1   **A translated name for the scroll** (for example, Exodus).

2   **The name of the scroll in Hebrew.**

3   **The scroll's classification number.** The traditional notation generally includes some or all of the following information: the number of the cave in which the fragment was uncovered; the location of the cave; the number assigned to the overall fragment; an abbreviated name; and the specific fragment number (for example, the classification number 4QpHos[a] would indicate Cave 4, Qumran, Pesher Hoshe'a, fragment a).

4   **Measurements of the fragment, in centimeters.**

5   **An approximation of the period in which the scroll was copied.**

6   **Diagram of the scroll** photograph to assist the reader in locating the transcribed portions.

7   **A description of the scroll.** Reference to the major publication of the fragment, as well as its transcription and translation, are located at the foot of the entry.

8   **On the pages following the image: a translation, as well as a transcription into Hebrew script of a portion of the text.** Translated and transcribed text enclosed in brackets indicates letters, words or passages reconstructed by the editor; in parentheses are additions deemed necessary for fluency.

The second section of the catalog, "From the Qumran Ruin," describes the archaeological artifacts. They are organized by material, such as pottery, wood, leather and textiles. Brief introductions and captions describe the materials and their uses.

From the Qumran Caves

Damascus Document

ברית דמשק

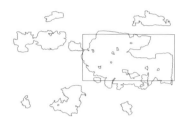

4Q266 (4QDᵃ)
10 x 26.5 cm
Copied late first century BCE

The Damascus Document circulated widely in the Qumran community, as evidenced by the number of fragments of the text found in caves 4, 5 and 6. The contents of these Qumran fragments are also found in two medieval manuscripts discovered by Solomon Schechter in 1896 in the genizah of the Ezra Synagogue in Old Cairo. The manuscripts from Egypt are often also called the "Cairo Document." The text of these documents describes a community which fled from Judea to Damascus.

The Damascus Document contains two major parts: a hortatory section and a legal section. The first part exhorts the congregation to remain faithful to the new covenantal community estab-

lished in the "Land of Damascus." Scholarly opinion is divided about the meaning of "Damascus," which could either refer to the Syrian city, or symbolize a place of exile. The legal section lists the statutes and rules for life in the community, and the regulations for the rituals, purification rites, and worship of the community.

Paleographically, this fragment is the earliest of the eight fragments of the Damascus Document uncovered in Cave 4, and can be dated to late first century BCE.

Reference: Baumgarten, J.M., *Discoveries in the Judean Desert XVIII: Qumran Cave 4.XIII: The Damascus Document* (Oxford: Clarendon Press, 1996). Florentino García-Martínez and Eibert J.C. Tigchelaar, *The Dead Sea Scrolls Study Edition*, 2 vols. (Leiden: E.J. Brill; Grand Rapids, Mich.: Wm. B. Eerdmans Publishing Co., 1997, 1998), pp. 588-89.

[. . .] וא[ם [שפל ה]שת [א]ו השפח[ת]   1

[מן העור . . . הכ]הן וראה הכהן אותו כמראי הבשר החי וכ[. . .]   2

[. . . צרעת] היאה האוחז}ת{ה בעור החי וכמשפט הזה   3

[. . .] וראה הכוהן ביום השביעי והנא נוסף מן החי   4

[אל המת . . . צ]רעת ממארת היא ומשפט נתק הרוש והזק[ן]   5

[. . .] וראה הכוהן וה]נא באה הרוח ברוש }ו{ᵃⁱ בזקן באוחז[ת]ה   6

בגיד ופר[ח הנגע מתחת הש]ער והפך מרא}ת{ה לדק צוהב כי כעשב   7

הוא אשר [י]ש הרחש תחתו vacat ויקיץ שורשו ויבש פרחו ואשר   8

אמר וצ'ה הכוהן וגלחו את ה}ב{ר'ש}ר{ ואת הנתק לא יגלחו למען אשר   9

י}ש{ספור הכוהן את השערות המיתות והחיות וראה אם יו}ש{סף מן   10

}כ{ החי אל המת בשבעת הימים טמא הואה ואם לו ליוסף מן הח[י]ות]   11

על המיתות והגיד נמלא [ד]ם ור[ו]ח החיים עולה וי'רדת בון[נרפא]   12

הנגע זה משפט [תור]ת הצרעת לבני אהרון להבדיל ל[. . .]   13

Damascus Document 4Q266 (4QDᵃ), fragment 6, column 1

1   [. . . But i]f [the] tumor or the ras[h is deeper]

2   [than the skin . . . the prie]st, and the priest sees in it something like living flesh, or like [. . .]

3   [. . .] it is [leprosy] which has taken hold of the living skin. And in accordance with this regulation,

4   [. . .] The priest shall examine it on the seventh day; if something live has been added

5   [to the dead, . . .] it is malignant [le]prosy. And the regulation for ringworm of the head or of the bear[d:]

6   [. . . the priest shall examine whe]ther the spirit has come into the head {and} /or/ the beard, taking hold of

7   the artery, and [the disease has] spro[uted from underneath the ha]ir, changing its appearance to yellowish —
    for it is like a plant

8   under which there [is] a worm, *blank* which cuts its root so that its fruit turns pale. And what he

9   said: *Lev 13:33* "The priest shall order them to shave their {flesh} head, but not to shave their ringworm,"
    it is so that

10 the priest can count the dead and living hairs, and see whether

11 living (hairs) have been added to the dead ones during the seven days, then he is impure; but if liv[ing] (hairs)
    have not been added

12 to the dead ones, and the artery is full of [blo]od, and the sp[ir]it of life goes up and down through it,

13 that disease [is healed]. This is the regulation of the law of leprosy for the sons of Aaron so that they can
    differentiate [. . .]

Community Rule

סרך היחד

4Q260 (4QS^f)
7.5 x 49 cm
Copied late first century BCE
— early first century CE

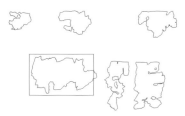

Originally known as the Manual of Discipline, the Community Rule contains regulations ordering the life of the members of the *yahad*, the group within the Judean Desert sect who chose to live communally. The rules of conduct, which are accompanied by admonitions and punishments to be imposed on violators, deal with the manner of joining the group, the relations between the members, their way of life and their beliefs. The sect divided humanity between the righteous and the wicked, and asserted that human nature and everything that happens in the world are irrevocably predestined. The scroll ends with songs of praise to God.

A complete copy of the scroll — 11 columns in length — was found in Cave 1, but 10 fragmentary copies were recovered in Cave 4 and a small section was found in Cave 5. The large number of manuscripts of this scroll, including the complete copy, attests to its importance for the sect.

The manuscript on display was copied between the late first century BCE and the early first century CE.

Reference: Alexander, P.S., and G. Vermes, *Discoveries in the Judean Desert XXVI: Qumran Cave 4.XIX: 4QSerekh Ha-Yahad and Two Related Texts* (Oxford: Clarendon Press, 1998). Florentino Garcia-Martinez and Eibert J.C. Tigchelaar, *The Dead Sea Scrolls Study Edition*, 2 vols. (Leiden: E.J. Brill; Grand Rapids, Mich.: Wm. B. Eerdmans Publishing Co., 1997, 1998), pp. 538-39.

55

[אר]חם על כול סוררי דרך לוא אנחם בנכוחים עד תום   1

ד[רכ]ם ובליעל לוא אשמור בלבבי ולוא ישמע בפי   2

נבלות וכחש עוון [ומ]רמות וכזבין לוא ימצאו בשפתי   3

ופרי קודש בלשוני vacat ושקוצים לוא ימצא   4

בה בהוד[ות אפתח vacat פי[ו]צדקות אל תס[פר]   5

לשוני תמ[י]ד ומעל [אנשים [עד ת]ום פשעם   6

Community Rule 4Q260 (4QS^f), column 5

1   [Shall I have mer]cy for all those who turn aside from the path. I shall not comfort the oppressed until their p[ath] is

2   perfect. I shall not retain Belial within my heart. From my mouth no

3   vulgarity shall be heard or wicked deceptions; sophistries or lies shall not be found on my lips.

4   The fruit of holiness will be on my tongue, *blank* profanity shall not be found

5   on it. With hymn[s shall I open] *blank* my mouth, [and] the just acts of God

6   my tongue will ev[er reco[unt] and the unfaithfulness] of men [until] their iniquity [is com]plete.

War Rule

סרך המלחמה

11Q14 (11QSM)
14.5 x 16 cm
Copied c. 20-50 CE

This fragment is part of a composition that describes the end of an eschatological war in which the leader of the evil Kittim (the Romans) was killed. It also tells of how the land was cleansed of contaminated enemy corpses and repentance from sin took place. The fragment on display is from the end of the text and contains a benediction, bestowing blessings on the eschatological community of Israel — probably the outcome of cleansing and repentance.

This fragment overlaps with a text recovered from Cave 4 that has been dubbed the "Pierced Messiah Text" (4Q285). Both of these fragments may well represent versions of the missing finale of the War Scroll from Cave 1, in which it is said that the forces of good and evil will clash on the battlefield "at the end of days." A major difference between the two lies in the identification of the central figure: 4Q285 deals with the "Prince of the Congregation," while the War Rule highlights the figure of the high priest.

The handwriting is the developed Herodian formal script of c. 20-50 CE.

Reference: García-Martínez, F., E.J.C. Tigchelaar and A.S. van der Woude, *Discoveries in the Judean Desert XXIII: Qumran Cave 11.II: 11Q2-18, 11Q20-30* (Oxford: Clarendon Press, 1998). Florentino García-Martínez and Eibert J.C. Tigchelaar, *The Dead Sea Scrolls Study Edition,* 2 vols. (Leiden: E.J. Brill; Grand Rapids, Mich.: Wm. B. Eerdmans Publishing Co., 1997, 1998), pp. 1210-11.

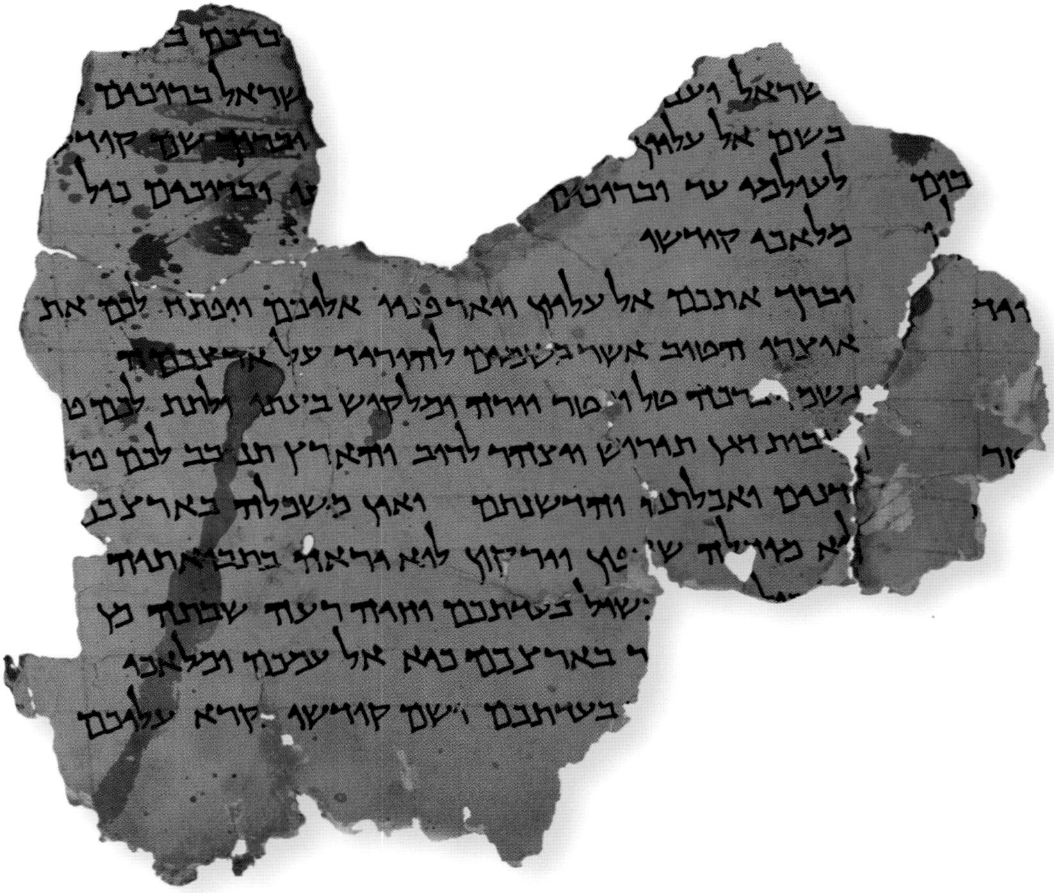

<table>
<tr><td>7</td><td>יברך אתכם אל עליון ויאר פניו אליכם ויפתח לכם את</td></tr>
<tr><td>8</td><td>אוצרו הטוב אשר בשמים להוריד על ארצכמה</td></tr>
<tr><td>9</td><td>גשמי ברכה טל ומטר יורה ומלקוש בעתו ולתת לכם פר[י]</td></tr>
<tr><td>10</td><td>תנובות דגן תירוש ויצהר לרוב והארץ תנובב לכם פרי</td></tr>
<tr><td>11</td><td>[ע]דנים ואכלתם והדשנתם vacat ואין משכלה בארצכם</td></tr>
<tr><td>12</td><td>ולוא מוחלה שדפון וירקון לוא יראה בתבואתיה</td></tr>
<tr><td>13</td><td>[ואין]כול[נגע ומ]כשול בעדתכם וחיה רעה שבתה מן</td></tr>
<tr><td>14</td><td>[הארץ ואין דב]ר בארצכם כיא אל עמכם ומלאכי</td></tr>
<tr><td>15</td><td>[קודשו מתיצבי]ם בעדתכם ושם קודשו נקרא עליכם</td></tr>
</table>

War Rule 11Q14 (11QSM), fragment 1, column 2

7   May God Most High bless you, may he show you his face, and may he open for you

8   his good treasure which is in the heavens, to cause to fall down on your earth

9   showers of blessing, dew and rain, early and late rains in their season, and to give you fru[it],

10   the harvests of wheat, of wine and of oil in plenty. And for you the land will yield [de]licious fruits.

11   And you shall eat (them) and be replete. *blank* In your land there will be no miscarriage

12   nor will one be sick; drought and blight will not be seen in its harvests;

13   [there will be no disease] at all [or stum]bling blocks in your congregation, and wild animals will vanish from

14   [the land. There will be no pesti]lence in your land. For God is with you and [his holy] angels

15   [are] in the midst of your Community. And his holy name is invoked over you

Thanksgiving Psalms הודיות

4Q427 (4QHª)
16 x 17.5 cm
Copied 75 BCE — end of the first
century BCE

The Thanksgiving Psalms *(Hodayot)* comprise a collection of about 30 poetic compositions. Modeled to some extent on the form of the biblical psalms of "individual thanksgiving," they express gratitude and praise for what God has done for the psalmist, especially in granting knowledge and insight, deliverance from distress, and membership in the community. In many of the psalms, a formulaic introduction has been preserved: "I thank you, O Lord, because..."; there is no set conclusion. In some psalms, there is a stronger sense of the individual speaking as one specially chosen to have a distinct role in instructing others; many scholars have suggested that these psalms were composed by the "Teacher of Righteousness." Other psalms have more focus on the community and contain extended reflections on human weakness and sinfulness and the greatness of divine grace and mercy.

There are eight copies of the *Hodayot,* arranged in different collections and orders. The best preserved manuscript — from Cave 1 at Qumran — was published by E. Sukenik in 1954 (1QHª). The six manuscripts from Cave 4, published in 1999, are more fragmentary. In the fragments from the Cave 4 manuscript displayed here, the psalms are arranged in a different order from 1QHª.

This copy of the *Hodayot* is written in a Hasmonean or early-Herodian semi-cursive hand and has been dated from 75 BCE to the end of the century.

Reference: Chazon, E., et al., in consultation with J. VanderKam and M. Brady, *Discoveries in the Judean Desert XXIX: Qumran Cave 4.XX: Poetical and Liturgical Texts, Part 2* (Oxford: Clarendon Press, 1999). Florentino García-Martínez and Eibert J.C. Tigchelaar, *The Dead Sea Scrolls Study Edition,* 2 vols. (Leiden: E.J. Brill; Grand Rapids, Mich.: Wm. B. Eerdmans Publishing Co., 1997, 1998), pp. 896-97.

Thanksgiving Psalms 4Q427 (4QHᵃ), fragment 7, column 1

13   . . . Sing, favored ones, sing to the king of

14   [glory, rejoice in the assem]bly of God, exult in the tent of salvation, praise in the [holy] residence,

15   [e]xalt together with the eternal host, ascribe greatness to our God and glory to our King;

16   [san]ctify his name with stalwart lips and powerful tongue, raise your voices in unison

17   [in a]ll periods, cause the sound of the shout to be heard, rejoice with everlasting happiness, and un-

18   ceasingly bow down in the united assembly. Bless the one who does amazing wonders, and shows the might

of his hand

Miqsat Ma'ase ha-Torah (Some Torah Precepts)

מקצת מעשה התורה

4Q394 (4QMMT)
16.5 x 17 cm
Copied late first century BCE —
early first century CE

This scroll is a sectarian polemical document, of which six incomplete manuscripts were discovered at Qumran. Most of the manuscripts are inscribed on parchment, although several papyrus fragments also have survived. Together, these fragments provide a composite text of about 130 lines, covering probably two-thirds of the original. The initial part of the text is completely missing.

The document, apparently in letter form, is unique in language, style and content. It probably consisted of four sections: the opening formula, now lost; a calendar of 364 days; a list of more than 20 rulings in religious law *(halakhot)*, most of which are peculiar to the sect; and an epilogue that deals with the separation of the sect from the multitude of the people and attempts to persuade the addressee to adopt the sect's legal views. The *halakhot* deal chiefly with the Temple and its ritual.

The author states that disagreement on these matters caused the sect to secede from Jerusalem. As the beginning of the text has been lost, the identities of both the author and the addressee are unknown. However, a commentary *(pesher)* to Psalm 37 relates that the "Teacher of Righteousness" conveyed a letter to his opponent, the "Wicked Priest." This could be a reference to this document, which is addressed to "the leader of Israel."

In general, the script belongs to the semi-formal tradition of Herodian times, indicating that this manuscript was copied at some time between the late first century BCE and the early first century CE.

Reference: Qimron, E., and J. Strugnell, *Discoveries in the Judean Desert X: Qumran Cave 4.V: Miqsat Ma'ase ha-Torah* (Oxford: Clarendon Press, 1994). Florentino García-Martínez and Eibert J.C. Tigchelaar, *The Dead Sea Scrolls Study Edition*, 2 vols. (Leiden: E.J. Brill; Grand Rapids, Mich.: Wm. B. Eerdmans Publishing Co., 1997, 1998), pp. 792-95.

Miqsat Ma'ase ha-Torah
(Some Torah Precepts)

[וא]ף על החרשים שלוא שמעו חוק [ומ]שפט וטהרה ולא   2

[ש]מעו משפטי ישראל כי שלוא ראה ולוא שמע לוא   3

[י]דע לעשות והמה באים לטה[ר]ת המקדש *vacat*   4

[ו]אף על המוצקות אנחנו אומר[ים] שהם שאין בהם   5

[ט]הרה ואף המוצקות אינם מבדילות בין הטמא   6

[ל]טהור כי לחת המוצקות והמקבל מהמה כהם   7

לחה אחת ואין להבי למחני הק[ו]דש כלבים שהם   8

אוכלים מקצת [ע]צמות המ[קד]ש[ׁ ו]הבשר עליהם כי   9

ירושלים היאה מחנה הקדש היא המקום   10

שבחר בו מכל שבטי [ישראל כי] ירושלים היא ראש   11

מ[חנות ישראל ואף על מטע]ת עצי המאכל[הנ]טע   12

[בארץ ישראל כראשית היא לכוה]נים ומעשר[הבקר]   13

[והצון לכוהנים הוא *vacat* ואף על הצ]רועים א[נחנו]   14

[אומרים שלוא יבואו עם טהרת הקו]דש כי [בדד]   15

[יהיו מחוץ לבית ואף כתוב שמעת שיג]לח [וכבס]   16

68

Miqsat Ma'ase ha-Torah, 4Q394 (4QMMT), fragment 8, column 4

2   [And al]so concerning the deaf who have not heard the law [and the pr]ecept and the purity regulation, and have not

3   [h]eard the precepts of Israel, for whoever neither sees nor hears, does not

4   know how to behave. But these are approaching the pu[ri]ty of the temple. *blank*

5   [And] also [concerning liquid streams: we say that in these there is no

6   [pu]rity, and also that liquid streams cannot separate impure

7   [from] pure, because the liquid of the liquid streams and their vessels is alike,

8   the same liquid. And one should not let dogs enter the h[o]ly camp, because

9   they might eat some of the [bo]nes from the temp[le with] the flesh on them. For

10 Jerusalem is the holy camp, it is the place

11 which he has chosen from among all the tribes of [Israel, since] Jerusalem is the head

12 of the ca[mps of Israel. And also concerning the plantati]on of fruit trees [pla]nted

13 [in the land of Israel, it is like the first-fruits, it is for the prie]sts. And the tithe of [the cattle]

14 [and the flocks is for the priests. *blank* And also concerning le]pers: w[e]

15 [say that they should not enter (a place) with ho]ly [purity], but [in isolation]

16 [they shall stay outside a house. And also it is written that from the moment he sh]aves [and washes]

Calendrical Document

משמרות

4Q325 (4QCalendrical Doc D)
6 x 10.6 cm
End of the first century BCE

Fragments of some 20 calendar-related compositions of various types were discovered at Qumran, mostly in Cave 4. The manuscript presented here illustrates the Covenanters' method of synchronizing the holy seasons — festivals, Sabbaths and the "first days of the month" — with the two annual one-week terms of service in the Temple of the priestly courses *(Mishmarot)* in a six-year cycle. The rotating system facilitated the reconciliation of the biblical roster of 24 courses (Chron. 24: 7-9) that served in the lunar year of 354 days to the Covenanters' solar calendar of 364 days (that is, 52 weeks), by having three courses serve for a third week each and two for an additional half-week.

Proper chronology was fundamental to the Covenanters' messianic-millenarian expectations, which derived from and depended on an accurately defined succession of periods in history. The correct execution of the priestly services, riveted to the progression of the holy seasons, played a vital role in this time system.

This composition originally enumerated the annual holy seasons over a period of six years, together with the names of the priestly courses that officiated on each of these days. Partly preserved are references to festivals known from biblical sources — the "Sacrifice of the Passover Lamb" and the "Waving of the First Sheaf" — and to "the first of the (second, third and sixth) month," as well as to the Covenanters' special festivals of the "First Wine (Grapes)," the "First Oil (Olives)" and the "Offering of the Wood (for the altar)," which are not explicitly recorded in the Bible.

References: Talmon, S., J. Ben-Dov and U. Glessmer, *Discoveries in the Judean Desert XXI: Qumran Cave 4.XVI: Calendrical Texts* (Oxford: Clarendon Press, 2001). Talmon, S., "A Calendrical Document from Qumran Cave 4 (*Mishmarot* D, 4Q325)," in *Solving Riddles and Untying Knots: Biblical, Epigraphic, and Semitic Studies in Honor of Jonas C. Greenfield,* ed. by Ziony Zevit, Seymour Gitin and Michael Sokoloff (Winona Lake, Ind.: Eisenbrauns, 1995), pp. 327-344. Florentino García-Martínez and Eibert J.C. Tigchelaar, *The Dead Sea Scrolls Study Edition,* 2 vols. (Leiden: E.J. Brill; Grand Rapids, Mich.: Wm. B. Eerdmans Publishing Co., 1997, 1998), pp. 698-701.

1   [. . .]שי בשמונה עשר בו שבת בו שבת ע]ל יויריב . . . [
2   [. . .]בערב בעשרים וחמשה בו שבת על ידעיה ועלי[ו]
3   [מועד] השעורים בעשרים וששה בו אחר שבת רוש החודש הש[ני]
4   [בששה בו] על ידעיה בשנים בו שבת חרים בתשעה בו שבת
5   [שעורים]בששה עשר בו שבת מלכיה בעשרים ושלושה ב[ו]
6   [שבת מי]מין בשלושים בו שבת הקוץ vacat רוש החודש
7   [vacat] vacat השלישי אחר שבת

Calendrical Document 4Q325 (4QCalendrical Doc D), fragment 1

1   [. . .] . . . On the eighteenth of it (the first month of the first year) is the sabbath o[f Jehoiarib . . .]

2   [. . .] in the evening. On the twenty-fifth of it the sabbath of Jedaiah; and [hi]s duty includes

3   [the festival of] the barley on the twenty-sixth of it, (on the day) after sabbath. The beginning of the se[cond] month

4   [on the sixth of it (i.e., the course)] of Jedaiah. On the second of it the sabbath of Harim. On the ninth of it the sabbath of

5   [Seorim.] On the sixteenth of it the sabbath of Malchiah. On the twenty-third of [it]

6   [the sabbath of Mija]min. On the thirtieth of it the sabbath of Hakkoz. *blank* The beginning of the

7   [*blank*] *blank* third month (on the day) after the sabbath . . .

Phylactery

תפילין

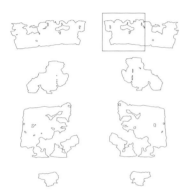

4Q138, 4Q136, 4Q134, 4Q143
(Phyl K, I, G, P)
7 x 11.6 cm
Copied first century CE

Qumran has provided us with the earliest remains of phylacteries (or *tefillin*), both the leather containers and inscribed strips of parchment. The command, "Bind them as a sign on your hand, fix them as an emblem on your forehead," (Deut. 6:8) was practiced by Jews from early times. In the Second Temple Period, the sages established that phylacteries would include four scriptural passages (Exod. 13:1-10, 13:11-16 and Deut. 6:4-9, 11:13-21) serving "as a sign and a reminder."

The phylactery texts were inscribed in clear minuscule characters on tiny strips of parchment which were worn on the left arm and on the forehead, a custom practiced by Jews to this day.

Some of the phylacteries found at Qumran deviate from the traditional passages prescribed by the sages. This variation, as well as other irregularities noted by scholars who have been studying the texts, led to the conclusion that at least some of the phylacteries are sectarian.

Phyl K bears the text of Deut. 10: 12-11:7 (recto) and Deut. 11:7-12 (verso), neither complying with the passages prescribed by the sages.

Phyl K is a copy dated to the first century CE.

Reference: de Vaux, R. and J.T. Milik, *Discoveries in the Judean Desert VI: Qumran Grotte 4.II: I. Archéologie; II: Tefillin, Mezuzot et Targums* [4Q128-4Q157] (Oxford: Clarendon Press, 1977).

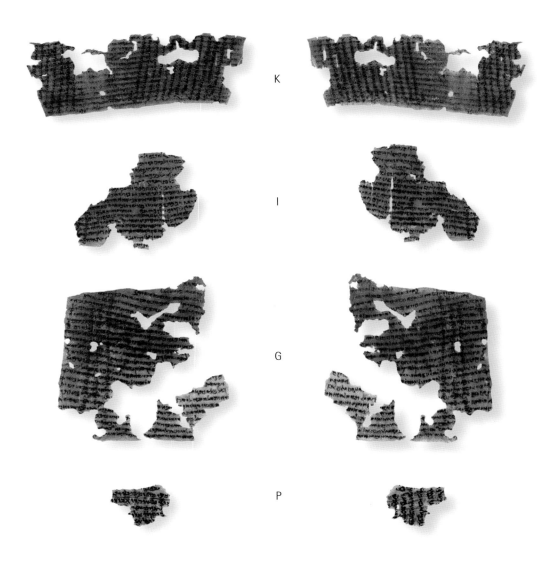

K

I

G

P

14   **עיניכמה** 11:7

15   **הראות את כו[ל] מ[עשי י] הוה הגדול**

16   **אשר עשה אתכמה** 11:8 **ושמרת ה**

17   **את כול המצוה אשר אנ( )וכי מצ**

18   **וכה היום למען תחזקו ועברתמה**

19   **ובתמה וירשתמה את הארץ אש**

20   **אתמה ע[וברי]ם את הירדן שמה**

21   **לרשת[ה** 11:9 **ול]מען תארכון ימים על**

22   **האדמ[ה א]שר נשבע יהוה לאבו**

23   **תכמה [לתת לה]מה ולזרעמה אחרי**

24   **[המ]ה ארץ [זב]ת חלב ודבש** 11:10 **כי הארץ**

25   **אשר אתמה באים שמה לרשתה לוא**

26   **כארץ מצרים היאה אשר יצאתה מ**

27   **שמה אשר תזרע את זרעכה והשק**

28   **[ב]רג[ליכה] כגן הירק**

Phylactery 4Q138 (Phyl K), verso, Deuteronomy 11:7-10

14   11:7 . . . For it is your own eyes that

15   have seen every great deed that the Lord

16   did. 11:8 Keep, then, this

17   entire commandment that I am commanding

18   you today, so that you may have strength to go in

19   and occupy the land that

20   you are crossing over (the Jordan)

21   to occupy, 11:9 and so that you may live long in

22   the land that the Lord swore to your ancestors

23   to give them and to their descendants,

24   a land flowing with milk and honey. 11:10 For the land

25   that you are about to enter to occupy

26   is not like the land of Egypt, from which you have come,

27   where you sow your seed and irrigate by foot

28   like a vegetable garden.

Nahum
Commentary

פשר נחום

4Q169 (4QpNah)
11 x 53 cm
Copied first century CE

The Nahum Commentary belongs to a literary genre which interprets the Scriptures with the intention of revealing allusions to current and future events. These events are related to the history of the Qumran sect, its leaders and its adversaries.

The biblical book of Nahum is a poem celebrating the destruction of Assyrian power in the fall of Nineveh. In this commentary, the sect interpreted the text in the light of the events of its own period. It is unusual, in that it mentions known historical figures, such as the Seleucid kings, Demetrius III and Antiochus IV, and the Hasmonean monarch, Alexander Jannaeus, who is called "the Lion of Wrath."

The commentary also mentions the tripartite division of Judaism of the time, referring to Ephraim (the Pharisees), Menasheh (the Sadducees) and Judah (the Essenes).

This text was composed in the
second century BCE; the manuscript
displayed here is a copy dating to
the first century CE.

Reference: Allegro, J.M. and A.A. Anderson,
*Discoveries in the Judean Desert V: Qumran
Cave 4.I* (Oxford: Clarendon Press, 1968).
Florentino García-Martínez and Eibert J.C.
Tigchelaar, *The Dead Sea Scrolls Study Edi-
tion*, 2 vols. (Leiden: E.J. Brill; Grand Rapids,
Mich.: Wm. B. Eerdmans Publishing Co., 1997,
1998), pp. 336-37.

1   [. . .] מדור לרשעי גוים אשר הלך ארי לבוא שם גור ארי

2   [ואין מחריד *vacat* פשרו על דמי]טרוס מלך יון אשר
     בקש לבוא ירושלים בעצת דורשי החלקות

3   [ולוא בוא כי לוא נתן אל את ירושלים]ביד מלכי יון
     מאנתיכוס עד עמוד מושלי כתיים ואחר תרמס

4   [. . .] *vacat* ארי טורף בדי גוריו [ו]מחנק ללביותיו טרף

5   [וימלא טרף חורה ומעונתו טרפה פשר הדבר] על כפיר החרון אשר יכה בגדוליו ואנשי עצתו

6   [את פתאי אפרים ואשר אמר וימלא טרף] חורה ומעונתו טרפה *vacat* פשרו על כפיר החרון

7   [אשר ימלא חורה רוב פגרי לעשות נק] מות בדורשי החלקות אשר יתלה אנשים חיים

8   [על העץ לפעול תועבה אשר לוא יעשה] בישראל מלפנים
     כי לתלוי חי על העץ [י]קרא הנני אלי[כה]

9   נא[ם יהוה צבאות והבערתי בעשן רובכ] ה וכפיריכה תאכל חרב והכר[תי מארץ ט]רפה *vacat*

10   ולא י[שמע עוד קול מלאכיכה *vacat* פש] רו רובכה הם גדודי חילו א[...]ם וכפריו הם

11   גדוליו[ואנשי עצתו ...] וטרפו הוא ההון אשר קב[צו כוה]ני ירושלים אשר

12   [י]תנוהו ע[... א]פרים ינתן ישראל [...] *vacat*

Nahum Commentary 4Q169 (4QpNah), fragments 3 & 4, column 1

1   [. . .] residence for the wicked of the nations. *Nah* ^{2:12} Where the lion went to go into it, a lion cub

2   [without anyone confining him. *blank* Its interpretation concerns Deme[trius, king of Yavan, who wanted to

    enter Jerusalem on the advice of those looking for easy interpretations,

3   [but he did not enter, for God had not given Jerusalem] into the hand of the kings of Yavan from Antiochus up

    to the appearance of the chiefs of the Kittim. But later, it will be trampled

4   [. . .] *blank Nah* ^{2:13} The lion catches enough for his cubs [and] strangles prey for his lionesses,

5   [and fills his cave with prey, and his den with spoil. The interpretation of the word] concerns the Angry Lion

    who struck (together) with his nobles and the men of his counsel

6   [the simple folk of Ephraim. And concerning what he says: *Nah* ^{2:13} "he fills] his cave [with prey] and his den

    with spoils," *blank* Its interpretation concerns the Angry Lion

7   [who filled his cave with a mass of corpses, carrying out rev]enge against those looking for easy interpretations,

    who hanged living men

8   [from the tree, committing an atrocity which had not been committed] in Israel since ancient times, for it is

    [hor]rible for the one hanged alive from the tree. *Nah* ^{2:14} See, I am against [you]!

9   Orac[le of YHWH of Hosts. I shall burn yo]ur [throng in the fire] and the sword will consume your cubs. [I will]

    eradica[te the sp]oils [from the earth], *blank*

10 and no [longer] will [the voice of your messengers be heard. *blank*] Its [interpre]tation: "Your throng" are his

    gangs of soldiers [. . .]; "his cubs" are

11 his nobles [and members of his council, . . .] and "his spoils" is the wealth which [the pries]ts of Jerusalem

    accu[mulated] which

12 they will deliver [. . . E]phraim, will be given Israel [. . .] *blank*

Enoch

חנוך

4Q212 (4QEn⁹ ar)
11.5 x 28 cm
Copied 50-1 BCE

The Book of Enoch is one of the most important Apocryphal works of the Second Temple Period. Enoch, the father of Methuselah, is mentioned only once in the Hebrew Bible (Gen. 5:21-24). According to the biblical narrative, Enoch lived for 365 years and "walked with God; then he was no more for God took him."

Rabbinic sources and pseudepigraphic literature attach many tales and legends to the figure of Enoch. He is all-wise, knowing the secrets of the universe, and is the source of information for natural and supernatural occurrences. The fullest portrait of Enoch emerges in 1 Enoch, a work preserved in its entirety on in Ge'ez (Classical Ethiopic).

The Book of Enoch is the earliest of the pseudepigraphic books. It is quoted in the Book of Jubilees and in the Testaments of the Twelve Patriarchs, and is referred to in the New Testament (Jude 1:14).

In all likelihood, the original language of most of this work was Aramaic, but the source text was lost in antiquity. Portions of a Greek translation were discovered in Egypt, and quotations are known from the Christian Church Fathers. The discovery of the texts from Cave 4 has finally provided parts of the Aramaic original, covering 1 Enoch. The text presented here is from the composition known as the Apocalypse of Weeks, including information about what will happen in the eighth, ninth and tenth weeks at the end of days.

The Qumran manuscripts of Enoch have been dated paleographically to some time between the early second century and the end of the first century BCE. This manuscript is a copy dated to 50-1 BCE.

Reference: Milik, J.T., *The Books of Enoch: Aramaic Fragments of Qumran Cave 4* (Oxford: Clarendon Press, 1976). Florentino Garcia-Martinez and Eibert J.C. Tigchelaar, *The Dead Sea Scrolls Study Edition*, 2 vols. (Leiden: E.J. Brill; Grand Rapids, Mich.: Wm. B. Eerdmans Publishing Co., 1997, 1998), pp. 444-45.

15 ומן בתרה יקום שביע תמיני קשוט דבה תתיה[ב חרב]

16 לכול קשיטין למעבד {דינא} דין קשוט מן כול רשיעין

17 ויתיהבון בידהון ועם סופה יקנון נכסין בקשוט

18 ויתבנא היכל [מ]ל[כ]ות רבא ברבות זוה לכול דרי עלמין

19 ומן בתרה שביע תשיעי וק[שוט וק]דין קשוט ו[ד]ין קשוט בה]יתגלא

20 לכול בני ארעא כלה וכול עב[די רשעיא יעברו]ן מן כול

21 ארעא כולה וירמון לבור[. . .]כלהון

22 לארח קשט עלמא ומן [. . . דבשבי]עה

23 דין עלמא וקץ דינא רבא[. . .] ושמין

24 קדמין בה יעברון ושמ[. . .]ין [ ] שמיא

25 צ[הר]ין ודנחין לכול עלמי[ן . . . ש]בעין שגי

26 [די לא]איתי סוף לכול מ[נינהון . . . וקש]טא יעבדון

15   After this, the eighth week will come, the one of justice, in which [a sword] will be giv[en]

16   to all the just, for them to carry out {the judgment} just judgment against the wicked

17   and they will be delivered into their hands. At its close, they will gain riches in justice

18   and there will be built the temple of the [k]in[g]ship of The Great One, in his glorious greatness, for all eternal generations.

19   And after that, the ninth week. [In it] will be revealed jus[tice and just] ju[dgment]

20   to all the sons of the whole earth. All those who ac[t wickedly will vanish] completely from the entire

21   earth and they shall be hurled into the [eternal] pit. All [men will see]

22   the just eternal path. And after [that, the tenth week. In] its [seven]th (part)

23   there will be eternal judgment and the moment of the great judgment [and he will carry out revenge

      in the midst of the holy ones.]

24   In it, the first heaven will pass away and [there will appear a new] hea[ven and all the forces of] heaven

25   will ri[se] and shine throughout all eternity, [seven times more. After that there will be] many [w]eeks

26   [the number of which will not] have an end [ever, in which] they shall practice [goodness and just]ice

Pseudo-Ezekiel

פסבדו יחזקאל

4Q386 (4QpsEzek[b])
10 x 24 cm
Second century BCE

This manuscript is one of five copies of a previously unknown composition found at Qumran. This writing reworks the canonical prophesies of Ezekiel, including the Vision of the Dry Bones (Ezek. 37) and the Vision of the Chariot (Ezek. 1). Especially interesting is this version of the Vision of the Dry Bones. It is understood to represent resurrection at the End of Days as the reward of the righteous. This is, then, the earliest extant witness to such an interpretation.

The best preserved fragment of Pseudo-Ezekiel is the manuscript displayed here. It shows the upper sections of three consecutive columns. The second column deals with a non-biblical vision that was revealed to Ezekiel about future events in Egypt relating to the people of Israel. The events and figures involved are enigmatic, and the entire passage is open to more than one interpretation.

Reference: Dimant, D., *Discoveries in the Judean Desert XXX: Qumran Cave 4.XXI: Para-Biblical Texts, Part 4: Pseudo-Prophetic Texts* (Oxford: Clarendon Press, 2001). Florentino Garcia-Martinez and Eibert J.C. Tigchelaar, *The Dead Sea Scrolls Study Edition*, 2 vols. (Leiden: E.J. Brill; Grand Rapids, Mich.: Wm. B. Eerdmans Publishing Co., 1997, 1998), pp. 774-77.

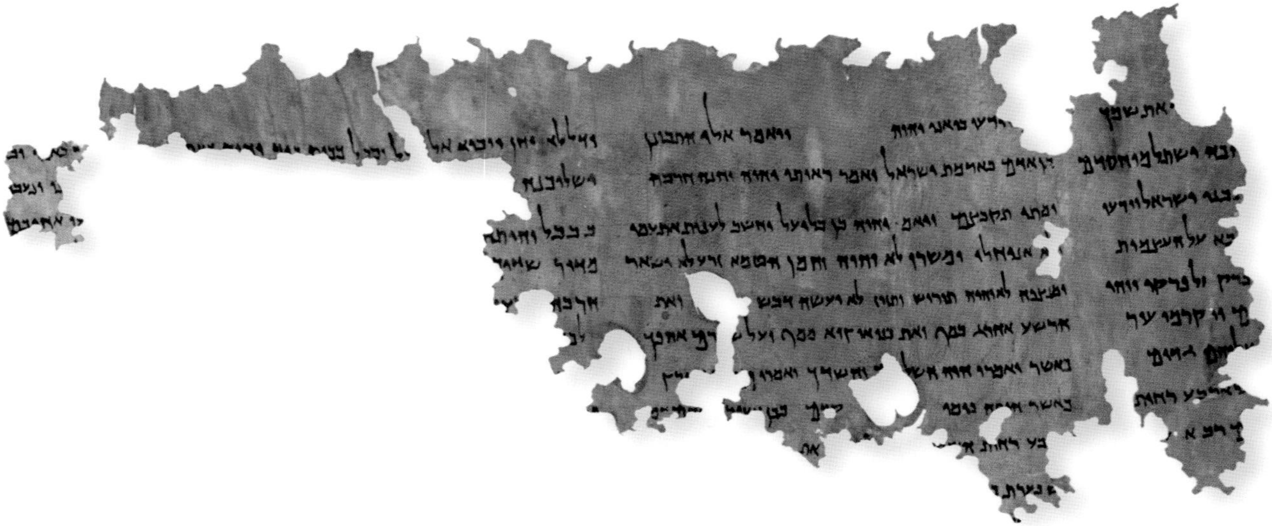

1 [. . .]. וידעו כי אני יהוה *vacat* ויאמר אלי התבונן

2 בן אדם באדמת ישראל ואמר ראיתי יהוה והנה חרבה

3 ומתי תקבצם ויאמר יהוה בן בליעל יחשב לענות את עמי

4 ולא אניח לו ומשרו לא יהיה והמן הטמא זרע לא ישאר

5 ומנצפה לא יהיה תירוש ותזיז לא יעשה דבש *vacat* [*vacat*] ואת

6 הרשע אהרג במף ואת בני אוציא ממף ועל ש[א]רם אהפך

Pseudo-Ezekiel 4Q386 (4QpsEzek^b), fragment 1, column 2

1   [. . .] And they will know that I am YHWH. *blank* And he said to me: "Consider,

2   son of man, the land of Israel." And I said: "I have seen, YHWH; behold it is desolate.

3   And when will you assemble them?" And YHWH said: "A son of Belial will plot to oppress my people,

4   but I will prevent him, and his dominion will not exist; but a multitude will be defiled, offspring will not remain.

5   And from the grapevine there will be no new wine, nor will the bee (?) make honey. *[blank] blank* And the

6   wicked man I will kill in Memphis and I will make my sons go out of Memphis: I will turn myself toward their re[mn]ant.

Exodus

שמות

4Q22 (4Qpaleo Exod^m)
31 x 21 cm
c. 100 BCE

On display is a scroll fragment of Exodus 6:25-7:19. The complete book of Exodus written in this script would have filled 57 columns. This manuscript is 43 columns in length and consists of chapters 6-37. The text of this Exodus manuscript is of an expanded textual tradition, which also formed the basis for the Samaritan text of Exodus.

The scroll is written in paleo-Hebrew script, an early form of Hebrew writing dominant in the First Temple period. Its occasional recurrence in the Second Temple period is considered a manifestation of nationalistic traits that survived through generations.

Hasmonean coinage of the first century BCE bears similar script. A characteristic of scrolls in paleo-Hebrew script seen here is the placement of the letter ו *vav* (which stands for the word "and") in open spaces between paragraphs, when the new paragraph should have opened with the ו *vav.*

The scroll is inscribed in a fine and consistent formal hand, which dates to c. 100 BCE.

References: Skehan, P., E. Ulrich and J. Sanderson, *Discoveries in the Judean Desert IX: Qumran Cave 4.IV: Palaeo-Hebrew and Greek Biblical Manuscripts,* with a contribution by P.J. Parsons (Oxford: Clarendon Press, 1992). Translation by Bastiaan Van Elderen.

2 [ ] הוא אהרון ומשה אשר ^{6:26}

3 [אמר יהוה] להם הוציאו את בנ[י] ישראל מארץ מצרים על

4 [צבא]תם ^{6:27} הם המדברים אל פרעה מלך מצרים להוציא את בני

5 [ישראל] ממצרים הוא משה ואהרון ^{6:28} ויהי ביום דבר

6 [יהוה] אל משה בארץ מצרים ^{6:29}

7 [ידבר] יהוה אל משה לאמור אני יהוה דבר אל פרעה מלך מצרים

8 [את כל א]שר אני דובר אליך ^{6:30} ויאמר משה לפני יהוה

9 [הן אני] ערל שפתים ואיך ישמע אלי פרעה ^{7:1} ויאומר

10 [יהוה]אל משה ראה נתתיך אלהים לפרעה ואהרון אחיך יהיה

11 [נביאך] ^{7:2} אתה תדבר את כל אשר אצוך ואהרון אחיך ידבר אל

12 [פרעה ושלח]את בני ישר[אל] [ו]אני אקשה את לב פרעה ^{7:3}

13 [והרביתי את א]תתי [וא]ת מופתי בא[ר]ץ מצרים

Exodus 4Q22 (4Qpaleo Exod^m), column 1, Exodus 6:26-7:3

2   6:26 It was this same Aaron and Moses to whom

3   the Lord said, "Bring the children of Israel from the land of Egypt by

4   their divisions." 6:27 It was they who spoke to Pharaoh king of Egypt to bring the children

5   of Israel out of Egypt, the same Moses and Aaron. 6:28 On the day when the Lord spoke

6   to Moses in the land of Egypt,

7   6:29 the Lord said to Moses saying, "I am the Lord; tell Pharaoh king of Egypt

8   all that I am speaking to you." 6:30 But Moses said in the presence of the Lord,

9   "I am unskilled in speaking, why would Pharaoh listen to me?"

10   7:1 And the Lord said to Moses, "See, I have made you like God to Pharaoh, and your brother Aaron shall be

11   your prophet. 7:2 You shall speak all that I command you, and Aaron your brother shall tell

12   Pharaoh to let the children of Israel go. 7:3 But I will harden the heart of Pharaoh,

13   and multiply my signs and wonders in the land of Egypt."

Psalms

תהילים

11Q5 (11QPs[a])
18 x 71.5 cm
30-50 BCE

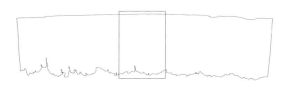

This impressive scroll is a liturgical collection of psalms and hymns, comprising parts of 41 biblical psalms in non-canonical sequence and with variations in detail from the canonical psalms. In addition to the biblical psalms, it presents non-canonical psalms, including five Syriac Apocryphal psalms. Also included is a prose passage about the psalms attributed to King David: "...And the total was 4,050. All these he (David) composed through prophecy, which was given him from before the Most High" (11QPs[a] 27:10-11).

This Psalms scroll, found in Cave 11 in 1956 and unrolled in 1961, is one of the longer texts from Qumran. Its surface is the thickest of any of the scrolls, and it may be calfskin rather than sheepskin (the writing material most commonly used at Qumran). It is written on the coarse grain side, instead of the smoother flesh side of the parchment.

The scroll contains 28 incomplete columns of text, five of which are displayed here. It is clear that six to seven lines are missing from the bottom of each column. The scroll's script is of fine quality, with the letters carefully fashioned in the Jewish bookhand style of the Herodian period (c. 37 BCE — 70 CE). On paleographic grounds, the manuscript is dated between 30 and 50 CE. Note that the Tetragrammaton (YHWH, the four-lettered divine name of God) is inscribed in the paleo-Hebrew script.

Reference: Sanders, J.A., *Discoveries in the Judean Desert IV: The Psalms Scroll of Qumran Cave 11 (11QPsa)* (Oxford: Clarendon Press, 1965). Translation by Bastiaan Van Elderen.

1   לדויד אודכה ^{138:1}

2   יהוה בכול לבי נגד יהוה אלוהים אזמרכה ^{138:2} אשתחוה

3   אל היכל קודשכה ואודה את שמכה על חסדכה ועל אמתכה

4   כי הגדלתה על כול שמכה אמרתכה ^{138:3} ביום קראתי ותענני

5   תרהיבני בנפשי עז ^{138:4} יודוך יהוה מלכי ארץ כי שמעו

6   אמרי פיך ^{138:5} וישירו בדרכי יהוה כי נדול כבוד יהוה

7   ^{138:6} כי רם יהוה ושפל יראה ונבה ממרחק יידע ^{138:7} אם אלך

8   בתוך צרה תחיני על אף אויבי תשלח ידכה ותושיעני

9   ימינכה ^{138:8} יהוה יגמור בעדי יהוה חסדכה לעולם

10 מעשי ידיכה אל תרף

Psalms 11Q5 (11QPsᵃ), Column 21, Psalm 138

1   ¹³⁸:¹ . . . of David. I will give you thanks,

2   O Lᴏʀᴅ, with all my heart, before the gods I sing your praise. ¹³⁸:² I bow down

3   toward your holy temple and give thanks to your name for your steadfast love and for your faithfulness,

4   for you have exalted your word above all your name. ¹³⁸:³ On the day I called, you answered me.

5   You made me bold with strength in my soul. ¹³⁸:⁴ All the kings of the earth shall give you thanks, O Lᴏʀᴅ,

     for they have heard the words of your mouth.

6   ¹³⁸:⁵ They shall sing of the ways of the Lᴏʀᴅ, for great is the glory of the Lᴏʀᴅ.

7   ¹³⁸:⁶ For though the Lᴏʀᴅ is high, yet he regards the lowly; but the haughty he perceives from afar. ¹³⁸:⁷ Though I walk

8   in the midst of trouble, you preserve me against the wrath of my enemies; you stretch out your hand and your right hand

9   saves me. ¹³⁸:⁸ The Lᴏʀᴅ will fulfill his purpose for me; O Lᴏʀᴅ, your steadfast love [is] forever.

10   The works of your hands do not forsake.

From the Qumran Ruin

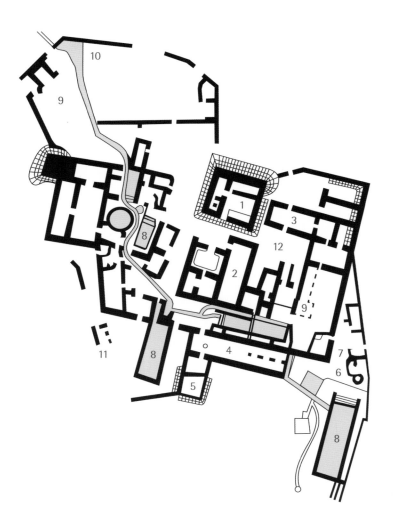

1   Tower
2   Scriptorium
3   Kitchen
4   Refectory
5   Larder
6   Kiln
7   Pottery workshop
8   Cisterns, ritual baths
9   Former ritual baths
10 Aqueduct
11 Stables
12 Courtyards

 water system

Stone Vessels

Stone vessels, usually made of easily workable soft limestone, were common in the Jerusalem area in the late Second Temple Period. Stone vessels of expert workmanship in a variety of shapes and sizes were found in abundance at Qumran.

It is evident that the use of stone vessels was extensive. The reason for their existence can be found in Jewish ritual law *(halakhah)*. Stone — as opposed to pottery — does not become ritually unclean. Jewish law maintains that pottery vessels that have become ritually unclean must be broken, never to be used again, whereas in similar circumstances stone vessels retain their ritual purity and need not be discarded.

Some of these vessels served the same functions as ceramic vessels, and some had particular shapes and functions. Although the raw material is common in Jerusalem, the cost of production was, no doubt, far greater than that of pottery. The widespread manufacture of stone vessels came to an end with the destruction of the Second Temple (70 CE).

Large goblet
Limestone
height: 72 cm

This vessel was produced on a lathe, probably in Jerusalem, and shows excellent crafts-manship. It is surprising that an ancient lathe was capable of supporting and work-ing such a large and heavy stone block.

Measuring cup
Limestone
height: 13 cm

Cylindrical cups of this type, ranging in height between 5 cm and 15 cm, are fre-quently found in sites of the Second Temple Period. It is believed that their capacities correspond to the dry and liquid measures mentioned in the Mishnah.

This vessel type was pared with a knife or chisel, and its surface was left unsmoothed. The vertical handles rule out the possibility that it might have been produced on a rotating lathe.

Pottery

Pottery, coins and written material found at an archaeological site allow for the establishment of a relative and an absolute chronological and cultural framework. Consequently, the pottery found in the Dead Sea area disclosed many facets of the Qumran story.

The vessels shown here are representative of the finds from the immediate area of Qumran. Items from the surrounding caves and openings in the cliffs are indistinguishable from those excavated at the Qumran site itself. Recent testing of the clay from these two groups of pottery shows their chemical composition to be identical. Qumran seems to have been a regional center — most likely, a single pottery workshop supplied the entire area.

Despite the large quantity of ceramic vessels found at Qumran, the repertoire is limited — apart from a large number of cylindrical scroll jars, it consists chiefly of modest items of daily use, such as juglets, flasks, drinking cups, cooking pots, serving dishes and bowls. A storeroom found during the excavation contained more than a thousand pottery items arranged by usage: vessels for cooking, serving, pouring, drinking and dining. Note the simple design of the pottery and the lack of ornamentation. These unadorned, functional vessels reflect the ascetic nature of the Qumran community.

References: de Vaux, R., *Archaeology and the Dead Sea Scrolls* (Oxford: Oxford University Press, 1973); Lapp, P., *Palestinian Ceramic Chronology, 200 BC - AD 70* (New Haven, Conn.: American Schools of Oriental Research, 1961).

Jars with lids
Pottery
height: 40–50 cm

Some of the Dead Sea Scrolls were found in
cylindrical pottery jars of this type, which are
unknown elsewhere. The discovery of these
singular vessels in the Qumran excavations
as well as in the caves has been considered
by many to be convincing evidence of the
link between the settlement and the caves
from the early days of Qumran research.
Recent scientific testing of the scroll jars
using Instrumental Neutron Activation
Analysis proves that the jars from the ruins
and those from the caves share the same
chemical fingerprint. These tests also deter-
mined that the clay from the jars matches
clay from the Qumran site, thus establishing
that the jars were produced locally.

Inkwell
Pottery
height: 5 cm
diameter: 5 cm

Two inkwells — one of pottery and another of bronze — were found at the Qumran excavations among the debris of a collapsed upper story. After careful reassembly, the debris proved to contain the remains of a low, smoothly plastered mudbrick table (about five meters long), two shorter tables and a bench. These findings suggested to the site's excavators that this was the location of a manuscript production center, known as a scriptorium. It is possible that many of the scrolls were written or copied by Qumran scribes, although a number of manuscripts of earlier date and other locations are also part of the Dead Sea Scrolls corpus.

The cylindrical pottery vessel above, missing the loop handles, has a flat base and a small, circular opening with a rim. This type of vessel also has been found in excavations in Jerusalem.

Plates, bowls and goblets
Pottery
diameter: 13.6—16.4 cm

Piles of plates, bowls and goblets were found in one of the rooms at Qumran. This room, probably a pantry, was located near the assembly room, which may have served as a dining room.

The wheel-made plates are shallow, with a ring base and upright rim. The firing is metallic. Hundreds of plates were recovered, most of them complete, and some bore traces of soot.

Dried Dates and pits

Food remains often are found in desert sites. They provide us with some insight into ancient diets. The most common food remains are date pits, olive stones and the shells of pomegranates and nuts.

Jugs and juglets
Pottery

Cooking pots, bowl and funnel
Pottery

Wooden Artifacts

Wooden artifacts are rare finds in the material culture of the ancient Near East, and few specimens from the Roman period have survived. The considerable quantity of organic finds coming from the Judean Desert is an exceptional occurrence, a result of the arid climatic conditions prevailing in the area. The finds include many wooden objects — bowls, boxes, mirror frames and handles, combs and spinning equipment — all contributing to the study of ancient woodworking techniques.

Combs
Boxwood
height: 5-6.1 cm
width: 6 cm

Similar to most ancient combs, these
boxwood combs are two-sided. One side has
closely spaced teeth for straightening hair.
The other side provides more teeth — for
delousing.

Bowl
Wood
diameter: 11 cm
height: 4.9 cm

This deep bowl with a flat ring base was expertly turned on a lathe. A ridge at the bottom creates a groove in the interior. The upright band-like rim has incisions at the top, on both the interior and exterior surfaces.

Bowl
Wood
diameter: about 13.5 cm
(part of the bowl is missing)
height: 6 cm

This deep bowl was also turned on a lathe.
It has a flat ring base and a thickened rim.
Three sets of double concentric incisions
decorate the exterior.

Basketry and Cordage

Basketry and cordage represent a major type of perishable material retrieved in the arid part of Israel. The basketry fragments on display are made of date palm leaves, a material convenient for making baskets and mats. The technique used is a type of plaiting that was popular during Roman times and remained in favor through the following centuries; a variant is still used in the Near East today.

Because of the exceptional conditions inside caves in the Dead Sea region, several baskets and mats of plaited weave survived intact. Their survival permitted the reconstruction of the Qumran plaited basket, made of a single plait composed of several elements and spiraling from base to rim. The coiled plait was not sewn together; instead, successive courses were joined around cords as the weaving progressed. In a complete basket, the cords are not visible, but they form horizontal ridges and a ribbed texture. Each basket has two arched handles made from palm-fiber rope. Much ingenuity is displayed by the way in which they were attached to the rims by passing reinforcing cords through the plaited part of the basket.

Basketware was probably very common, as it is today, in household activities. However, in times of need, baskets and mats also served for collecting and wrapping the bones and skulls of the dead.

The medium-thick ropes on display may have been used in packing and tying bundles and waterskins. The compound cables made of plied cords possibly served as handles.

Tamar Schick

Basket fragments
Palm leaves
length: 13–14 cm
width: 21–23.5 cm

Ropes and cables
Palm leaves, palm fibers
and undetermined rushes
diameter: 6-16 mm

Leather Objects

The Judean Desert has yielded a fair number of leather objects, permitting study of ancient tanning techniques. Waterskins, large bags, pouches, purses, sandals and garments have been found in varied desert sites.

The majority of leather objects are of sheepskin. A few pieces, particularly those used as patches, are of goat- and calfskin. The skins were vegetable-tanned, mostly with gall and pomegranates.

Exhibited here are sandal soles of the *solea* type, found in the Qumran area. These soles are made of two layers of leather secured with leather bindings. Tabs entered the upper sole, through slits situated near the heel. The upper part of each tab (non-existent in the sandals on display) usually was pierced by two vertical slits, through which the main strap was threaded. The two ends of the main strap were then threaded into a slit near the toe, where they were tied, holding the foot onto the sole. Decorative intersecting incisions on the upper soles also may have had a practical purpose.

Sandals
Leather
length: 23.5–24 cm

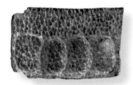

Phylactery Cases
Leather

Phylacteries *(tefillin)* are small, square boxes worn on the left arm and forehead. They serve as a sign and a reminder that the Lord brought the children of Israel out of Egypt (Exod. 13:9, 16). The command, "Bind them as a sign on your hand, fix them as an emblem on your forehead" (Deut. 6:8), was practiced by Jews from early times, and the tradition continues to this day.

In the Second Temple Period, the sages established that phylacteries would include four scriptural passages inscribed on parchment placed in a box-like container. Qumran has provided us with the earliest remains of the leather containers and the inscribed parchments.

Type A
dimensions: 1 × 2-3 cm

This phylactery case has two parts stitched together. It is a four-compartment case, to be worn on the head. Each compartment held a minute roll.

Type B
dimensions: 2.2 × 1.2 cm

Worn on the arm, this case has only one compartment. It is formed of a single piece of leather folded in two, with one half deeply stamped out to form a cavity to hold a minute roll. A fine leather thong was inserted at the middle, and the halves were folded over and stitched together.

Leather Scroll Fasteners

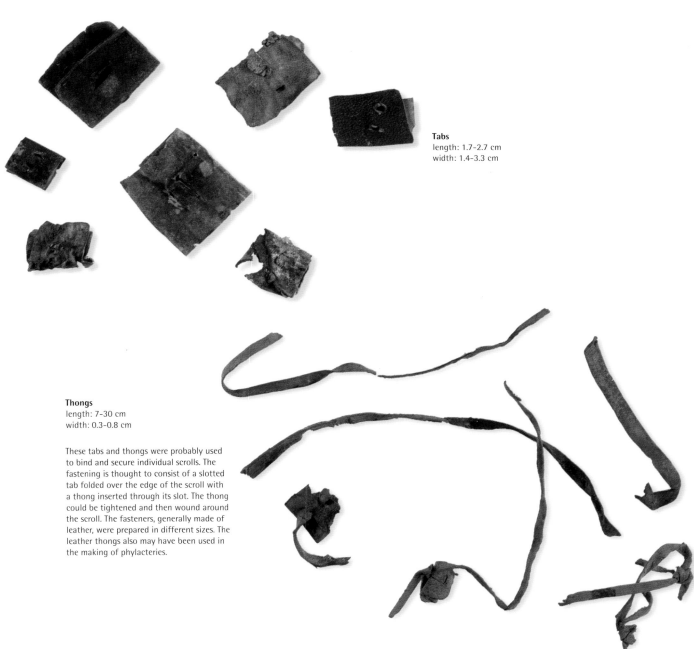

Tabs
length: 1.7–2.7 cm
width: 1.4–3.3 cm

Thongs
length: 7–30 cm
width: 0.3–0.8 cm

These tabs and thongs were probably used to bind and secure individual scrolls. The fastening is thought to consist of a slotted tab folded over the edge of the scroll with a thong inserted through its slot. The thong could be tightened and then wound around the scroll. The fasteners, generally made of leather, were prepared in different sizes. The leather thongs also may have been used in the making of phylacteries.

Textiles and Spinning Equipment

The textile on display is one of many pieces found in 1949 in some of the Qumran caves. The pieces appear to have come from small cloths, ranging in size from 57 x 60 cm to 27 x 23 cm. They usually have one or two cut edges, hinting that the original loom-woven cloth was larger and wider. The cut edges were rolled and whipped. The yarn is S-spun, the proper way to spin flax, with consideration for the natural twist of the fibers. The linen is usually of fair quality in an even linen weave. The majority of the cloths are plain, although some have a fringe, with or without an open space at the end of the cloth. Several cloths have a corded starting border, indicating a somewhat primitive loom, possibly the warp-weighted loom or the two-beamed vertical loom. The only form of colored decoration, although rare, is thin bands, usually two weft lines each, of indigo-dyed linen threads. Sometimes, as in the piece on display, the rolled edge is oversewn with a blue thread.

It seems probable that all the cloths from Qumran are associated in one way or another with the scrolls. Some of them certainly were scroll wrappers; the remains of one scroll were found wrapped in a small square of linen. Other cloths, found folded into pads, may have formed packing for worn-out scrolls inside the jars. Still other pieces — with corners twisted or tied around with linen cord — were probably protective covers, tied over the jars' tops. A few deteriorated textiles show repairs and patching (see the textile on display).

Materials related to spinning — spindles, shafts and whorls — have also been found. Spinning involves both drawing out the fibers of the raw material and twisting them into thread. The spindle usually consists of a stick or a shaft and a flywheel or spindle-whorl of some weight, giving momentum. Shafts, which were usually made of wood, have rarely survived; whorls, of such durable materials as stone, clay, bone, ivory and glass, are more common finds in excavations.

Tamar Schick

Reference: G.M. Crowfoot in Barthélemy O.P., D. and J.T. Milik, *Qumran Cave I* (Oxford: Clarendon Press, 1955).

Cloth with patch
Linen
length: 27 cm
width: 21 cm

One edge of this cloth is cut, folded and
whipped with a two-ply blue thread. The
other edges are torn, with some frayed
edges. On the light beige background of
the plain woven cloth are four thin, light
blue bands.

Spindle and whorls
Wood
length of shaft: 23.5 cm
diameter of shaft: 0.9 cm
height of whorls: 0.9 cm
diameters of whorls: 0.5-1 cm

Hoard of coins

In the 1955 season of excavations at Qumran, three intact ceramic vessels containing 561 silver coins were found under a doorway. The vessels were filled to the brim with coins, and the mouth of one of the vessels was covered with a palm-fiber stopper.

Père Roland de Vaux, excavator of Qumran, relied heavily on the coin evidence for his dating and inter-pretations of the various phases of the site. The early coins in the hoard were Seleucid *tetradrachms* of the third quarter of the second century BCE, minted in Tyre, as well as six Roman Republican coins from the middle of the first century BCE. The bulk of the hoard represents the autonomous continuation of the Seleucid mint: the well-known series of Tyrian *shekalim* and half-*shekalim*, minted from 126/125 BCE onwards. These are the same coins that were prescribed in the Temple for the poll tax and other payments. The latest coins in the hoard date to 9/8 BCE.

Two of the three hoard vessels are of a type otherwise unknown in the ceramic repertoire at Qumran. De Vaux suggested that the hoard corroborated the information in the Community Rule, which relates that new adherents in the sect were to surrender their worldly goods to the treasurer of the community. The vessels' contents would then constitute the deposit of one or a number of new adher-ents. A second possibility is that the hoard was the collection of half-*shekalim* toward some future payment of a Temple tax.

Exhibited here are 18 *shekalim*, half-*shekalim* and *denars* minted between 133 and 10/9 BCE.

Donald T. Ariel

References: de Vaux, R., *Archaeology and the Dead Sea Scrolls* (Oxford: Oxford University Press, 1973); Magness, J., "Two Notes on the Archaeology of Qumran," in *Bulletin of the American Schools of Oriental Research* 312 (1998), pp. 37-44.

Hoard Of Coins
Silver
diameter: 1.9-2.8 cm

Shekalim and half-*shekalim*, part of a hoard of 561 coins found in vessels under a doorway at Qumran.

Resources

Glossary

Bastiaan Van Elderen

Aaron The first high priest of the Hebrews and the brother of Moses (see Exodus 4.14). Only the descendants of Aaron served as ritual priests.

Alexander the Great (356-323 BCE) The king of Macedonia (336-323 BCE) who conquered the Greek city-states and the Persian Empire from Asia Minor and Egypt to India.

Antioch The capital of the Seleucid Empire (c. 300-64 BCE). It was located at modern Antakya in southern Turkey. As an important city in the Roman Empire, it was the base of Paul's missionary work.

Antiochus III ("the Great," 242-187 BCE) The king of Syria (223-187 BCE) who extended the Seleucid Empire south to Palestine. Invading Asia Minor, he fought against the Romans by whom he was defeated in Greece (191 BCE) and Asia Minor (190 BCE).

Antiochus IV (died 164 BCE?) The king of Syria (174-164 BCE) who provoked the revolt of the Maccabees (167 BCE) by attacking Jerusalem and desecrating the temple.

Apocalyptic A genre of religious literature in which otherworldly secrets about the nature of God, the heavens, and the impending "end times" are divulged. These texts purportedly were revealed in visions, dreams, and special revelations, often given by angels, and arose in times of crisis, especially during the Second Temple Period. See also **eschatology**.

Apocrypha Technically, the books included in the Septuagint (Greek) translation of the Hebrew Bible but not in the Hebrew text. More loosely, the term refers to extra-biblical books composed in the Second Temple Period. Most of these books, written primarily by Jewish authors, are included in Catholic and Orthodox Bibles but excluded from Jewish and Protestant Bibles.

Aramaic A branch of the northwest Semitic languages that is closely related to Hebrew and was used extensively in the Middle East after the Babylonian Exile. It was the lingua franca in Palestine in the Second Temple Period. About 20% of the Dead Sea Scrolls are written in Aramaic.

Asia Minor In ancient usage, a vast plateau between the Black Sea and the Mediterranean Sea, roughly equivalent to western and central modern Turkey.

Assyria An ancient empire in southwest Asia (Mesopotamia) whose greatest extent was from Egypt to the Tigris River and the Persian Gulf in 750-612 BCE. During this period the Assyrians frequently invaded Palestine.

Babylonian Captivity From 597 BCE (the fall of King Jehoiachin) to 586 BCE (the destruction of Jerusalem and the First Temple) the Babylonians frequently deported Judaeans to Babylonia. This period of exile of the Judaeans in Babylonia ended with the return of the exiles in 538 BCE.

Bactria An ancient country in western Asia between the Oxus River and the Hindu Kush mountains.

Bar Kokhba Literally, "son of the star," the designation of Simeon ben Kosiba, who led the Second Jewish Revolt against Rome in 132-135 CE.

Bar Kokhba Revolt The second revolt of the Jews against Rome, which took place in 132-135 CE.

Before the Common Era Abbreviated to BCE, an alternate designation for BC.

Belial Term meaning "worthlessness," "wickedness," or "destruction," used as the ancient Hebrew personification of lawlessness; i.e., the devil, Satan.

Benediction The act of uttering a blessing or the advantage conferred by blessing; a mercy or benefit.

Canon The collection of sacred literature accepted and considered as inspired and authoritative by a given religious community.

Canonization The process by which a religious community determines and delimits a body of literature as its authoritative and sacred Scriptures.

Common Era Abbreviated to CE, an alternate designation for AD.

Concordance An alphabetical index of the words of a document or book, with a reference to the passage in which each occurs and usually some part of the context.

Corpus A body of texts or manuscripts that have been grouped together, either in antiquity or by modern scholars.

Damascus The capital of Syria, in the southwestern part of the country, reputed to be the oldest continuously existing city in the world.

Dead Sea A lake between Israel and Jordan that is the lowest point on earth, at about 1350 feet below sea level. The Dead Sea is ten times saltier than the world's oceans, and is unable to support any aquatic life other than tiny microorganisms.

Dead Sea Scrolls A collection of ancient religious literature, including biblical manuscripts, largely written in Hebrew and Aramaic with a few texts in Greek. Dating from the late 3rd century BCE – 70 CE, this collection was discovered in the late 1940's in caves near the northwest shore of the Dead Sea.

denarius (pl. **denarii**) A Roman Republican coin, originally cast in silver and equivalent to a worker's average daily wage.

Deuteronomy The fifth book of the Pentateuch in the Hebrew Bible, containing a second statement of the Mosaic law.

Diaspora Greek term meaning "dispersion," referring to the Jewish population outside Palestine.

Edom An ancient region between the Dead Sea and the Gulf of Aqaba, bordering ancient Palestine, called Idumaea in Greek.

Ein Feshkha An area about 2 miles south of Qumran on the Dead Sea shore where brackish and sweet springs are located. In the surrounding agricultural area, excavations have uncovered ruins, including an industrial complex where some believe animal skins were processed into parchment.

End of Days A biblical term that later Jewish tradition understood to refer to the messianic era.

Enoch a) The father of Methuselah (Gen 5.18-24). b) The elder son of Cain (Gen 4.17f). c) The name of a pseudepigraphical book written in the intertestamentary period.

Ephraim The younger son of Joseph (Gen 41.52).

Eschatology The branch of religious study and belief dealing with various aspects of the End of Days, the messianic era, the afterlife, the final judgment, bodily resurrection, immortality of the soul, etc.

Essenes A sect of Jews in ancient Palestine, first appearing in the 2nd century BCE, distinguished by its withdrawal from the mainstream of society to establish a religious community with strict piety and ascetic ideals. As one of the religious movements of Jews during the Second Temple Period, the Essenes were a separatist group that formed an ascetic, esoteric, communal society with unique sacrificial and purity requirements. In response to apocalyptic visions, the sectarians retreated to the wilderness. Many scholars identify the sect of the Dead Sea Scrolls as a modified form of the Essenes.

Ethiopic The ancient Semitic language of Ethiopia.

exegesis The critical explanation or interpretation of a text, especially of sacred literature.

Ezekiel A 6th century BCE major Hebrew prophet and the author of one of the prophetic books in the Hebrew Bible.

Ezra A 5th century BCE Hebrew scribe and priest who, with Nehemiah, led the Hebrew exiles in their return to Palestine under the edict of Cyrus the Great as recounted in the Book of Ezra in the Hebrew Bible.

First Jewish Revolt The Jewish rebellion against Roman rule that began in 66 CE and ended in 73 CE with the Roman capture of the Zealot fortress at Masada. Its climax occurred with the destruction of Jerusalem and the Second Temple in 70 CE.

First Temple The temple erected by Solomon in Jerusalem in c. 950 BCE which was destroyed by the Babylonians in 586 BCE. The term First Temple Period designates the period during which this temple stood.

Ge'ez The classical form of the ancient Ethiopic language, still used today in Ethiopian liturgy.

Gemara As the latter of the two sections of the Jewish Talmud, this is a commentary on the Mishnah.

Genizah (Heb. "storeroom") This was a store-room in a synagogue for worn out, damaged or defective Hebrew writings and ritual articles which cannot be destroyed because of their holiness. The famous genizah, discovered in 1895 in the ancient synagogue in Cairo, yielded a treasure of Second Temple, rabbinic, and medieval texts.

halakhah (pl. **halakhot**) The part of Jewish traditional literature which dealt with Jewish ritual and civil laws and texts related to them (in contrast to haggadic texts, which dealt with theological or devotional matters). Disagreement on these matters apparently caused the Dead Sea Scrolls community to withdraw to the desert.

Hagiographa (Gr. "holy writings") The third of the three divisions of the Hebrew Bible, also called Ketubim (Heb. "the writings"). This division contains the Psalms, Proverbs, Job, Song of Solomon, Ruth, Lamentations, Ecclesiastes, Esther, Daniel, Ezra, Nehemiah, 1 and 2 Chronicles, variously arranged. Later this term was used for literature about the lives of saints and venerated persons.

Hasidim Hebrew for "pious ones," a loosely organized group of pietists known from the Maccabean Period through Mishnaic times. Devoted to strict observance of the law and opposed to the adoption of aspects of Greek culture, they were forerunners of both the Pharisees and the Essenes.

Hasmonean Dynasty The descendants of the Maccabeans who ruled Palestine from 152 to 63 BCE after the Maccabean Revolt in c. 167 BCE. Included in the dynasty are Judas Maccabaeus, Jonathan, Simon, John Hyrcanus, Aristobolus I, Alexander Jannaeus, Alexandra Salome, Hyrcanus II, and Aristobobus II.

Hellenistic Culture The amalgamation of Greek and native Near Eastern cultures that swept over the entire Near East in the wake of Alexander the Great's conquest c. 332-323 BCE.

Herodian Relating to Herod the Great (37–4 BCE), his family, or its supporters.

Hillel A Pharisee (60 BCE – 9 CE) of Babylonian origin, an authority on Judaic written and oral tradition and its interpretation.

Hodayot Thanksgiving psalms.

Intercalation The addition of an extra month to the lunar year in order to adjust it more closely to the solar year. To compensate partially for the fact that the lunar year is 11 days shorter than the solar year, the rabbis would intercalate a month at the end of the year twice in every seven years in order to keep the various feasts in their proper season.

Jerusalem The center of Jewish, Christian, and Islamic history, religion, and culture. As the capital of ancient Israel it was the location of the First Temple (built by Solomon) and the Second Temple (built by the returning exiles and enlarged and embellished by Herod the Great).

Jubilees, Book of One of the Pseudepigrapha (*vide infra*), dated in the 2nd century BCE, which is a rewriting of Genesis and part of Exodus. Twelve manuscripts of this document have been identified in the Qumran Library.

Judah The fourth son of Jacob and Leah whose descendants became the powerful tribe of Judah. After the division of the kingdom of Israel after Solomon, it was the name of the kingdom of the tribes of Benjamin and Judah in southern Palestine.

Jude A short book in the New Testament written by Jude, "a brother of James" (and possibly of Jesus).

Judea The name given to the southern part of Palestine during the Roman Period.

Judean wilderness or desert The low-lying desolate area of Judea south of Jerusalem and west of the Dead Sea. This arid region with limited rainfall was the area where the Dead Sea Scrolls were found along the northwest shore of the Dead Sea.

khirbeh/khirbet An Arabic term used to describe a low-lying mound of ruins of ancient occupation(s); e.g. Khirbet Qumran.

Kittim A place name in the Aegean Islands, perhaps Kition in Cyprus, that in the Dead Sea Scrolls is a code word for "Romans." The name referred originally to inhabitants of Kiti, capital of Cyprus, then to any Cypriots, later to Greeks in general, and eventually to Romans.

Late Antiquity The period between the rise of Alexander the Great (c. 330 BCE) and the Muslim conquest (c. 638 CE).

Levite A descendant of Levi, one of the sons of Jacob, and a member of the Israelite tribe of Levi, which was responsible for the maintenance of the Temple ritual and sacrificial system. The Aaronic priests belonged to this tribe.

Leviticus The third book of the Hebrew Bible, containing laws relating to the work of the priests and Levites in the performance of Jewish religious ceremonies and rituals.

Maccabean Revolt The revolt of the Jews led by the Maccabean family against the Seleucid rulers of Syria in 168-164 BCE. This victory of the Jews is celebrated on the holiday of Hanukkah.

Maccabees The family of Judas Maccabeus, the early leader of the revolt against the Seleucid ruler Antiochus Epiphanes. This priestly Jewish family, also known as the Hasmonaean dynasty, ruled Palestine in the 2nd and 1st centuries BCE (164-67 BCE).

Masada A fortress located on the southwest shore of the Dead Sea held by the Zealots during the First Jewish Revolt. The destruction of this site by the Romans in 73 CE brought to an end to this revolt and the Second Temple Period.

Masoretic Text The traditional, authoritative text of the Hebrew Bible, considered as such by Jews from mishnaic times until the present.

Memphis Ancient capital of (Lower) Egypt, now a ruined city on the Nile, south of Cairo.

mezuzah (pl. **mezuzot**) A manuscript of specific biblical verses which affirm God's sovereignty over the world and the obligations to observe his law. Mezuzot are affixed to the doorpost of Jewish homes in accord with the command of the Torah (Deut 6.8f). Eight mezuzot have been found in the Qumran caves.

midrash (pl. **midrashim**) (Heb. "expounding") A rabbinic method of biblical interpretation which employed a variety of techniques (e.g., allegories, word plays, gematria) to determine the meaning of a text. A midrash may be halakhic (legal, procedural) or haggadic (non-legal, illustrative, devotional).

miqveh (pl. **miqva'ot**) A ritual bath used for purification ceremonies by immersion in Judaism. Ten have been identified at Qumran.

millenarian Of or relating to a thousand, especially the thousand years of the prophesied millennium.

millennium The period of "a thousand years"" (a phrase variously interpreted) during which Christ is to reign on earth in Jerusalem, according to the prophetic statement in Rev 20.1-7.

mishmarot The 24 courses into which the Jewish priests were divided (cf. 1 Chr 24.7-19). The rotation of these groups according to the solar calendar is discussed in a number of Qumran calendrical texts.

Mishnah The great collection of rabinic halakhic (legal and procedural) material arranged and edited by Rabbi Judah ha-Nasi ("the Prince") (135-220 CE). It is divided into 6 orders containing a total of 63 tractates.

monotheism The doctrine or belief that there is only one god.

Nahum A late 7th century BCE Hebrew prophet whose name is identified with one of the Minor Prophets in the Hebrew Bible.

Nevi'im See the Prophets.

New Testament The collection of 27 books that were produced by the early Christian church and added to the Hebrew Bible to form the Christian Bible.

Nineveh The ancient capital of Assyria whose ruins today are opposite Mosul on the Tigris River in northern Iraq.

Old Testament The name given to the first of the two main divisions of the Christian Bible. In the Protestant Bible it equals the Hebrew Bible, whereas in the Catholic and Orthodox Bibles the apocryphal books are added.

oral law A second Torah (law), consisting of interpretations of the written Torah which was studied and passed down by oral tradition. In rabbinic Judaism it is believed that this oral Torah was given by God at Sinai with the written Torah and thus constitutes the authoritative interpretation of the written law.

Glossary

ossuary A small box, usually limestone, used as a receptacle for the bones of the deceased, used in burial practices in 1st century Palestine.

ostracon (pl. **ostraca**) A piece of broken pottery (a potsherd) used in ancient times as the writing surface for a short text or quick note.

paleo- A prefix meaning "old," "ancient."

paleography The comparative study of the shapes of letters in manuscripts and inscriptions in order to establish a history and chronology of scripts for the dating of documents.

Pentateuch The first five books of the Hebrew Bible, also called the Torah or the Five Books of Moses.

pesher (pl. **pesherim** or **pesharim**) (Heb. "interpretation") The unique biblical interpretations and commentaries of the Dead Sea sect which interpreted the words of the Hebrew Bible, especially the prophetic books, as referring to the experiences of the sectarians at Qumran in the Second Temple Period.

Pharisees A group of Hasidic Jews in the Second Temple Period who were the spiritual forebears of the talmudic rabbis. By strictly adhering to oral and written tradition, the Pharisees rigidly observed the rituals and ceremonies of Judaism. At the time of Josephus (1st century CE) the Pharisees were the largest of the various sects in Judaism.

Phoenicians An ancient maritime country on the northeast coast of the Mediterranean Sea which, though never being a major power, had significant relations with and influence on ancient civilizations in the area.

the Prophets The books which form the second of the three divisions of the Hebrew Bible, comprising a) Joshua, Judges, 1 and 2 Samuel, and 1 and 2 Kings; b) Isaiah, Jeremiah, and Ezekiel (major prophets); c) Hosea, Joel, Amos, Obadiah, Jonah, Micah, Nahum, Habakkuk, Zephaniah, Haggai, Zechariah, and Malachi (minor prophets). Group a) is called the Former Prophets; groups b) and c) together the Latter Prophets.

phylacteries (Heb. **tefillin**) Small leather boxes, usually square, which contained biblical texts in minuscule script. These were tied to the forehead and on the left arm, as commanded by Moses in. Deut 6.8 — "Bind them as a sign on your hand, fix them as an emblem on your forehead." As practiced by some Jews to this day, this is a reminder that God in ancient times led Israel out of Egypt. In the Qumran caves 30 phylacteries, the oldest to date, have been found. The text in these at times deviates from the later traditional Masoretic text and the passages differ from those prescribed by the rabbis.

Prayer of Jonathan This manuscript, of which only a fragment survives (4Q448), contains the apocryphal Psalm 154 (also in the Psalms Scroll from Cave 11 [11QPsa]) and a prayer for the welfare of King Jonathan, who has been identified by many scholars with Alexander Jannaeus, the Hasmonaean ruler (104-76 BCE).

pseudepigrapha Books written in the Second Temple Period but ascribed to an ancient biblical saint to give the document status and authority. The Qumran library contains some of the previously known texts and a number of additional similar texts.

pseudo- A prefix meaning "false," "deceptive." This prefix is used for some Qumran documents which are reworkings of canonical books. E.g., pseudo-Ezekiel is a reworking of the canonical Ezekiel.

Ptolemies The rulers of Egypt and its empire in the Hellenistic Period after the conquest of Alexander the Great.

Qumran (Khirbet Qumran) The area along the northwest shore of the Dead Sea where the Dead Sea Scrolls were found in eleven caves in bluffs and in the cliff face to the west. On a plateau in the area the ruins of a building complex were uncovered. This was the headquarters of the religious movement which produced and used the scrolls. The area is 33 miles north of Masada, about 8 miles south of Jericho and about 20 miles from Jerusalem.

rabbi (Heb. "my master," "my teacher") This term refers to a teacher or judge of the Jews of Palestine in the Roman and Byzantine Periods. The rabbis who shaped the texts of talmudic Judaism are collectively termed "the Rabbis."

rabbinic Judaism The form of Judaism that became accepted from the 2nd century CE on. As successors of Pharisaic Jews, rabbinic Jews accept the validity of oral tradition, beliefs in angels and spirits, and the resurrection of the dead.

ritual purity In Judaism this is the special state of cleanness required of those who would observe the laws of the Pentateuch relating to the pure and impure and take part in various religious ceremonies. Practices included avoidance of impure things and observance of various kinds of washing and other rituals for purification.

Sabbath The seventh day of the week (Saturday) as the day of rest and observance among the Jews.

sabbatical The designation for every seventh year, in which the Bible commands the remission of debts and prescribes leaving the land fallow.

Sadducees A sect of Second Temple Judaism which was connected primarily with the priestly aristocracy and accepted the authority of teaching based strictly on the Bible (written tradition) and its interpretation. The term derives from Zadok, the high priest at the time of Solomon. Since they were linked to the aristocracy and the Temple establishment, the Sadducees increasingly declined after the destruction of the Second Temple in 70 CE.

Samaritan The language spoken by the Samaritans (*vide infra*).

Samaritans A mixed people inhabiting central Palestine which descended from those original Israelites who were not exiled in 722 BCE and mingled with tribes introduced into the area by the Assyrians. The Samaritans maintained belief in the holiness of the Pentateuch to the exclusion of other writings deemed holy by the Jews and included in the Hebrew Bible. Their center was Neapolis (modern Nablus where a colony still exists today) and they offer sacrifices on nearby Mt. Gerizim.

scriptorium A room in a monastery or religious community where manuscripts were written or copied.

Second Temple The temple in Jerusalem, built by returning Jewish exiles in the early 6th century BCE and enlarged and embellished by Herod the Great, which was in use until its destruction by the Romans in 70 CE.

Second Temple Period (ca. 520 BCE - 70 CE) The period of the Second Temple in Jerusalem (from its construction by the returning Jewish exiles to its destruction in 70 CE). The Dead Sea Scrolls were composed, transcribed, and/or copied during this period.

sect (adj. sectarian) A group of persons with peculiarities of faith and practice differing from the mainstream body adhering to the same general system. Within Second Temple Judaism there were sectarian movements, such as the Pharisees, Sadducees, Essenes (Qumran?), and Zealots.

Seleucids After his death, Alexander the Great's empire was divided amongst his generals. Syria and surrounding areas were given to Seleucus I Nicator, the founder of the dynasty that ruled this area in Hellenistic times (312-64 BCE). At its height, the Seleucid Empire extended from the southern coast of modern Turkey, south through Palestine, and east to India's border.

Septuagint The Greek translation of the Hebrew Bible initiated by Ptolemy II Philadelphus (Egyptian ruler 285-246 BCE) and produced in Egypt in the 3rd and 2nd centuries BCE. As the first vernacular translation of the Hebrew Bible, it also included apocryphal books (most of which are included in the Catholic and Orthodox Bibles).

serekh A collection of laws or regulations, as found in a number of manuscripts at Qumran, identified in the collection as S ("rule").

stratigraphy The method of ordering and dating layers of soils and rock formations based on their composition and contents as found and identified in the course of an archaeological excavation. Artifacts found in the various strata often provide data for the dating of an individual stratum.

Syriac A dialect of Aramaic that was widely used in Syria and Mesopotamia from late pre-Christian antiquity until largely displaced by Arabic. It is still used in some Eastern Orthodox churches today.

Glossary

Ta'amireh The tribe of Bedouins who lived in the area along the western shore of the Dead Sea whose members found the first Dead Sea Scrolls.

tabernacle The tent used by the Israelites as a portal sanctuary until the construction of the Temple by Solomon. Its construction is prescribed in the book of Exodus, 25-27.

Talmud (adj. Talmudic) The authoritative body of rabbinic Jewish literature which contains the Mishnah and the Gemara, the literary results of the rabbinic discussions of Jewish law and tradition from the 2nd to 5th centuries CE. Codified in the 5th century, it is preserved in two traditions — Palestinian Talmud and Babylonian Talmud.

Targum The Aramaic paraphrases of the Hebrew biblical books. The term usually refers to the so-called Targum Onqelos of the Pentateuch.

Teacher of Righteousness The leader, perhaps the founder, of the Qumran sect. It may also refer to succeeding leaders of the community.

Tefillin See **phylacteries**.

Tetragrammaton The four-lettered name of God (JHWH, YHWH) in the Hebrew Bible which the Jews did not pronounce because of their great reverence for the name. They instead read the more general name "Lord" (*adonai*).

Torah (Heb. "instruction," "teaching") The first five books of the Hebrew Bible, also called the Pentateuch, which are traditionally ascribed to Moses. In rabbinic times the term was used more generally for Jewish law, both oral and written.

Transliterate To change letters, words, and/or phrases into corresponding characters of another alphabet or language.

Tyre An ancient seaport of Phoenicia and one of the great cities of antiquity which was famous for its navigators and traders in the Mediterranean Sea.

wadi The Arabic term for the channel or bed of a watercourse which is dry except during periods of rainfall. The Hebrew term for this seasonal stream or river is *nahal*.

Wicked Priest A Hasmonean priestly leader who had confrontation(s) with the Qumran Teacher of Righteousness and was considered by the Qumran sect as its archenemy.

Yahad (Heb. "unity," "oneness," "community") The term used in the Qumran literature to describe the pious group of sectarians living communally in the Qumran area who composed and/or copied the scrolls. The sectarians divided humanity between the righteous ("the sons of light" = themselves) and the wicked ("sons of darkness") and believed that God irrevocably predestined everything that happens in the world.

Zadok (adj. Zadokite) Zadok was one of the high priests of King Solomon in the 10th century BCE. The Zadokite priestly line dominated the high priesthood for most of Jewish history. Antiochus Epiphanes deposed the Zadokites, and the Hasmonaeans assumed the high priesthood. Not being of the Zadokite line, the Hasmoneans were considered unqualified to assume the office by some, including the Qumran sectarians.

Zealots As a more political than religious sect, the Zealots opposed Roman rule over the Jews. This cumulated in the First Jewish Revolt (66-70 CE) in which the Jews achieved independence. After the fall of Jerusalem in 70 CE the Zealots occupied Masada where they held out against the Romans until 73 CE.

Zion A term with various meanings in the biblical literature: a) a hill or mount of Jerusalem, the site of David's royal residence and the temple as the center of Hebrew national culture, government, and religion; b) the Israelites; c) the ancient Hebrew theocracy or the modern church of God; d) heaven as the final gathering place of true believers, the heavenly Jerusalem.

Contributors

Donald T. Ariel
Timothy J. Chester
Shuka Dorfman
Ellen Middlebrook Herron
Lena Libman
Ruth Peled
Tamar Schick
Pnina Shor
Ayala Sussmann
Emanuel Tov
Bastiaan Van Elderen
James C. VanderKam

Selected Bibliography

Official series

Discoveries in the Judaean Desert (DJD) (Oxford: Clarendon Press, 1955-).

I: Barthélemy O.P., D. and J.T. Milik, *Qumran Cave I*, 1955, xi + 163 pp. + xxxvii plates.
II, IIa: Benoit O.P., P., J.T. Milik, and R. de Vaux, *Les Grottes de Murabb'ât*, 1961, xv + 314 pp. + cvii plates.
III, IIIa: Baillet, M., J.T. Milik, and R. de Vaux, *Les "Petites Grottes" de Qumran*, 1962, xiii + 315 pp. + lxxi plates.
IV: Sanders, J. A., *The Psalms Scroll of Qumran Cave 11 (11QPsa)*, 1965, xi + 97 pp. + xvii plates.
V: Allegro, J.M. and A.A. Anderson, *Qumran Cave 4.I (4Q158-4Q186)*, 1968, xii + 111 pp. + xxxi plates.
VI: de Vaux, R. and J.T. Milik, *Qumran Grotte 4.II: I: Archéologie; II: Tefillin, Mezuzot et Targums (4Q128-4Q157)*, 1977, xi + 91 pp. + xxviii plates.
VII: Baillet, M., *Qumran Grotte 4.III (4Q482-4Q520)*, 1982, xiv + 339 pp. + lxxx plates.
VIII: Tov, E. with the collaboration of R.A. Kraft, *The Greek Minor Prophets Scroll from Nahal Hever (8HevXIIgr), (The Seiyâl Collection I)*, 1990, x + 169 pp. + xx plates.
IX: Skehan, P., E. Ulrich and J.E. Sanderson, *Qumran Cave 4.IV: Palaeo-Hebrew and Greek Biblical Manuscripts*, 1993, xiii + 250 pp. + xlvii plates.
X: Qimron, E. and J. Strugnell, *Qumran Cave 4.V: Miqsat Ma'ase ha-Torah*, 1994, xiv + 235 pp. + viii plates.

XI: Eshel, E., et al., in consultation with J. VanderKam and M. Brady, *Qumran Cave 4.VI: Poetical and Liturgical Texts, Part I*, 1998, xi + 473 pp. + xxxii plates.
XII: Ulrich, E., F.M. Cross, et al., *Qumran Cave 4.VII: Genesis to Numbers*, 1994 (repr. 1999), xv + 272 pp. + xlix plates.
XIII: Attridge, H., et al., in consultation with J. VanderKam, *Qumran Cave 4.VIII: Parabiblical Texts, Part 1*, 1994, x + 470 + xliii plates.
XIV: Ulrich, E., F. M. Cross, et al., *Qumran Cave 4.IX: Deuteronomy, Joshua, Judges, Kings*, 1995 (repr. 1999), xv + 183 pp. + xxxvii plates.
XV: Ulrich, E., et al., *Qumran Cave 4.X: The Prophets*, 1997, xv + 325 pp. + lxiv plates.
XVI: Ulrich, E., et al., *Qumran Cave 4.XI: Psalms to Chronicles*, 2000, xv + 302 pp. +.xxxviii plates.
XVII: Cross, F.M., D. W. Parry and E. Ulrich, *Qumran Cave 4.XVII: 1-2 Samuel*, 2002, ? + xxvii plates.
XVIII: Baumgarten, J. M., *Qumran Cave 4.XVII: The Damascus Document (4Q266-273)*, 1996, xix + 236 pp. + xlii plates.
XIX: Broshi, M., et al., in consultation with J. VanderKam, *Qumran Cave 4.XIV: Parabiblical Texts, Part 2*, 1995, xi + 267 pp. + xxix plates.
XX: Elgvin, T., et al., in consultation with J.A. Fitzmyer, S.J., *Qumran Cave 4.XV: Sapiential Texts, Part 1*, 1997, xi + 246 pp. + xviii plates.
XXI: Talmon, S., J. Ben-Dov and U. Glessmer, *Qumran Cave 4.XVI: Calendrical Texts*, 2001, xii + 263 + xiii plates.

XXII: Brooke, G., et al., *Qumran Cave 4.XVII: Parabiblical Texts, Part 3*, 1997, xi + 352 pp. + xxix plates.
XXIII: García-Martínez, F., E.J.C. Tigchelaar and A.S. van der Woude, *Qumran Cave 11.II: 11Q2-18, 11Q20-30*, 1998, xiii + 487 pp. + liv plates.
XXIV: Leith, M. J. W., *Wadi Daliyeh I: The Wadi Daliyeh Seal Impressions*, 1997, xxv + 249 pp. + xxiv plates.
XXV: Puech, É., *Qumran Cave 4.XVIII: Textes Hébreux (4Q521-4Q528, 4Q576-4Q579)*, 1998, xii + 229 pp. + xv. plates.
XXVI: Alexander, P., and G. Vermes, *Qumran Cave 4.XIX: 4Q Serekh Ha-Yahad and Two Related Texts*, 1998, xvii + 253 pp. + xxiv plates.
XXVII: Cotton, H. M. and Ada Yardeni, *Aramaic, Hebrew, and Greek Documentary Texts from Nahal Hever and other Sites, with an Appendix Containing Alleged Qumran Texts, (The Seiyâl Collection II)*, 1997, xxvii + 381 pp. + 33 figures and lxi plates.
XXVIII: Gropp, D. M., *Wadi Daliyeh II: The Samaria Papyri from Wadi Daliyeh*; E. Schuller et al., in consultation with J. VanderKam and M. Brady, *Qumran Cave 4.XXVIII: Miscellanea, Part 2*, 2001, xv + 254 pp. + lxiii plates.
XXIX: Chazon, Esther, et al., in consultation with J. VanderKam and M. Brady, *Qumran Cave 4.XX: Poetical and Liturgical Texts, Part 2*, 1999, xiii + 478 pp. + xxviii plates.
XXX: D. Dimant, *Qumran Cave 4.XXI: Parabiblical Texts, Part 4: Pseudo-Prophetic Texts*, 2001, xiv + 278 pp. + xii plates.

XXXI: Puech, É., *Qumran Grotte 4.XXII: Textes Araméens, Première Partie: 4Q529-549*, 2001, xviii + 439 pp. + xxii plates.

XXXII: Flint, P.W. and E. Ulrich, *Qumran Cave 1.II: The Isaiah Scrolls*, forthcoming.

XXXIII: Pike, D. and A. Skinner, in consultation with J. VanderKam and M. Brady, *Qumran Cave 4.XXIII: Unidentified Fragments*, 2001, xv + 376 pp. + xli plates.

XXXIV: Strugnell, J., D. J. Harrington and T. Elgvin, in consultation with J.A. Fitzmyer, S.J., *Qumran Cave 4.XXIV: 4QInstruction (Musar leMevin): 4Q415 ff.*, 1999, xvi + 584 pp. + xxxi plates.

XXXV: Baumgarten, J., et al., *Qumran Cave 4.XXV: Halakhic Texts*, 1999, xi + 173 pp. + xii plates.

XXXVI: Pfann, S., *Cryptic Texts;* P. Alexander, et al., in consultation with J. VanderKam and M. Brady, *Qumran Cave 4.XXV: Miscellanea, Part 1*, 2000, xvi + 739 pp. + xlix plates.

XXXVII: Puech, É., in consultation with J. VanderKam and M. Brady, *Qumran Cave 4.XXVII: Textes Araméens, Deuxième Partie: 4Q550-575, 580-582*, forthcoming.

XXXVIII: Charlesworth, J., et al., in consultation with J. VanderKam and M. Brady, *Miscellaneous Texts from the Judaean Desert*, 2000, xvii + 250 pp. + xxxvi plates.

XXXIX: Tov, Emanuel, ed., *The Texts from the Judaean Desert: Indices and an Introduction to the Discoveries in the Judaean Desert Series*, 2001/2, x + 452 pp.

Secondary text sources and English translations

Abegg Jr., Martin G., Peter Flint, and Eugene Ulrich, *The Dead Sea Scrolls Bible: The Oldest Known Bible, Translated for the First Time into English* (San Francisco: Harper San Francisco, 1999).

Burrows, M., J.C. Trever, and W.H. Brownlee, eds., *The Dead Sea Scrolls of St. Mark's Monastery. Vol. I: The Isaiah Scroll and the Habakkuk Commentary* (New Haven, Conn.: American Schools of Oriental Research, 1950).

Burrows, M., J.C. Trever, and W.H. Brownlee, eds., *The Dead Sea Scrolls of St. Mark's Monastery. Vol. II: Plates and Transcription of the Manual of Discipline* (New Haven, Conn.: American Schools of Oriental Research, 1951).

Charlesworth, James H., ed., *The Dead Sea Scrolls: Hebrew, Aramaic and Greek Texts with English Translations* (Louisville, Ky.: Westminster John Knox Press, 1994-).

A Facsimile Edition of the Dead Sea Scrolls: Prepared with an Introduction and Index by Robert H. Eisenman and James M. Robinson (Washington, D.C.: Biblical Archaeology Society, 1991).

García-Martínez, Florentino, *The Dead Sea Scrolls Translated: The Qumran Texts in English* (2nd edn) (Leiden: E.J. Brill, 1997).

García-Martínez, Florentino and Eibert J.C. Tigchelaar, *The Dead Sea Scrolls Study Edition*, 2 vols. (Leiden: E.J. Brill; Grand Rapids, Mich.: Wm. B. Eerdmans Publishing Co., 1997, 1998).

Lim, Timothy, ed., *The Dead Sea Scrolls Electronic Reference Library*, vol. 1 [CD-ROM] (Oxford; New York: Oxford University Press; Leiden: Brill Academic, 1997).

Scrolls from Qumran Cave 1: The Great Isaiah Scroll, the Order of the Community, the Pesher to Habakkuk (Jerusalem: Albright Institute of Archaeological Research, 1972).

Tov, Emanuel with Stephen J. Pfann, eds., *The Dead Sea Scrolls on Microfiche [Microform]: A Comprehensive Facsimile Edition of the Texts from the Judean Desert*, printed catalog by Stephen Reed (Jerusalem: Israel Antiquities Authority; Leiden: E.J. Brill, 1993).

Vermes, Geza, *An Introduction to the Complete Dead Sea Scrolls* (Minneapolis, Min.: Fortress Press, 1999).

Vermes, Geza, *The Complete Dead Sea Scrolls in English* 5th edn. (New York: Penguin Press, 1997).

Wacholder, Ben Zion and Martin G. Abegg, Jr., eds., *A Preliminary Edition of the Unpublished Dead Sea Scrolls: The Hebrew and Aramaic Texts from Cave Four* (Washington, D.C.: Biblical Archaeology Society, c1991-1996).

Wise, M., M. Abegg, and E. Cook, *The Dead Sea Scrolls: A New Translation* (New York: HarperCollins Publishers, 1999).

Yadin, Yigael, ed., *The Scroll of the War of the Sons of Light Against the Sons of Darkness*, trans. by Batya and Chaim Rabin (London: Oxford University Press, 1962).

Selected bibliography

Yadin, Yigael, ed., *The Temple Scroll: English & Hebrew* (Jerusalem: Israel Exploration Society, 1977-1983).

Studies

Boccaccini, Gabriele, *Beyond the Essene Hypothesis: The Parting of the Ways between Qumran and Enochic Judaism* (Grand Rapids, Mich.: Wm. B. Eerdmans Publishing Co., 1998).

Charlesworth, James H., ed., *Caves of Enlightenment: Proceedings of the American Schools of Oriental Research Dead Sea Scrolls Jubilee Symposium [1947-1997]* (N. Richland Hills, Tex.: BIBAL Press, 1998).

Charlesworth, James H., ed., *The Hebrew Bible and Qumran* (N. Richland Hills, Tex.: BIBAL Press, 2000).

Charlesworth, James H., ed., *Jesus and the Dead Sea Scrolls* (New York: Doubleday, 1992).

Charlesworth, James H., *The Pesharim and Qumran History: Chaos or Consensus?* (Grand Rapids, Mich.: Wm. B. Eerdmans Publishing Co., 2002).

Charlesworth, James H., ed., *Qumran Questions* (Sheffield, England : Sheffield Academic Press, c1995).

Collins, John J., *Apocalypticism in the Dead Sea Scrolls* (London; New York: Routledge Press, 1997).

Collins, John J. and Robert A. Kugler, eds., *Religion in the Dead Sea Scrolls* (Grand Rapids, Mich.: Wm. B. Eerdmans Publishing Co., 2000).

Cross, Frank Moore, *The Ancient Library of Qumran*, 3rd edn. (Minneapolis, Minn.: Fortress Press, 1995).

Cross, Frank Moore, "The Development of the Jewish Scripts, " in *The Bible and the Ancient Near East: Essays in Honor of William Foxwell Albright,* revised edition, ed. by G.E. Wright (New York: Doubleday, 1995).

Cross, Frank Moore and Shemaryahu Talmon, eds., *Qumran and the History of the Biblical Text* (Cambridge, Mass.: Harvard University Press, 1975).

Davila, James R., *Liturgical Works.* Eerdmans Commentaries on the Dead Sea Scrolls (Grand Rapids, Mich.: Wm. B. Eerdmans Publishing Co., 2000).

De Vaux, Roland, *Archaeology and the Dead Sea Scrolls* (London: Oxford University Press, 1973).

Dimant, Devorah and Uriel Rappaport, eds., *The Dead Sea Scrolls: Forty Years of Research* (Leiden; New York: E.J. Brill, 1992).

Evans, Craig A. and Peter W. Flint, eds., *Eschatology, Messianism, and the Dead Sea Scrolls* (Grand Rapids, Mich.: Wm. B. Eerdmans Publishing Co., 1997).

Fitzmyer, Joseph A., *The Dead Sea Scrolls and Christian Origins* (Grand Rapids, Mich.: Wm. B. Eerdmans Publishing Co., 2000).

Fitzmyer, Joseph A., *The Dead Sea Scrolls: Major Publications and Tools for Study*, rev. ed. (Atlanta, Ga.: Scholars Press, 1990).

Fitzmyer, Joseph A., *Responses to 101 Questions on the Dead Sea Scrolls* (New York: Paulist Press, 1992).

Flint, Peter W., ed., *The Bible at Qumran: Text, Shape and Interpretation* (Grand Rapids, Mich.: Wm. B. Eerdmans Publishing Co., 2001).

Flint, Peter W. and James C. VanderKam, eds., *The Dead Sea Scrolls After Fifty Years: A Comprehensive Assessment* (Leiden; Boston: E.J. Brill, 1998).

García-Martínez, Florentino and Julio Trebolle Barrera, *The People of the Dead Sea Scrolls,* trans. by Wilfred G.E. Watson (Leiden; New York: E.J. Brill, 1995).

Hodge, Stephen, *The Dead Sea Scrolls: An Introductory Guide* (London: Piatkus, 2001).

Kugel, James, *The Bible as It Was* (Cambridge, Mass.: Belknap Press of Harvard University Press, 1997).

Lim, Timothy H., ed., *The Dead Sea Scrolls in Their Historical Context* (Edinburgh: T. & T. Clark, 2000).

Magness, Jodi, *The Archaeology of Qumran and the Dead Sea Scrolls* (Grand Rapids, Mich.: Wm. B. Eerdmans Publishing Co., 2002).

Parry, Donald W. and Eugene Ulrich, eds., *The Provo International Conference on the Dead Sea Scrolls: Technological Innovations, New Texts, and Reformulated Issues* (Leiden; Boston: E.J. Brill, 1999).

Pearlman, Moshe, *The Dead Sea Scrolls in the Shrine of the Book* (Jerusalem: Israel Museum Products Ltd., c1988).

Reed, Stephen A., *The Dead Sea Scrolls Catalogue: Documents, Photographs and Museum Inventory Numbers* (Atlanta, Ga.: Scholars Press, 1994).

Roitman, Adolfo, ed., *A Day at Qumran: The Dead Sea Sect and its Scrolls* (Jerusalem: The Israel Museum, 1997).

Scanlin, Harold, *The Dead Sea Scrolls and Modern Translations of the Old Testament* (Wheaton, Ill.: Tyndale House Publishers, Inc., 1993).

Schechter, Solomon, *Documents of Jewish Sectaries: Edited from Hebrew MSS. in the Cairo Genizah Collection, Now in the Possession of the University Library, Cambridge* (New York: KTAV Publishing House, 1970).

Schiffman, Lawrence H., Emanuel Tov and James C. VanderKam, eds., *The Dead Sea Scrolls Fifty Years After Their Discovery: Proceedings of the Jerusalem Congress, July 20-25, 1997* (Jerusalem: Israel Exploration Society in cooperation with The Shrine of the Book, Israel Museum, 2000).

Schiffman, Lawrence H. and James C. VanderKam, eds., *Encyclopedia of the Dead Sea Scrolls* (New York: Oxford University Press, 2000).

Schiffman, Lawrence H., *Reclaiming the Dead Sea Scrolls* (Philadelphia: Jewish Publication Society, 1996).

Shanks, Hershel, ed., *Understanding the Dead Sea Scrolls: A Reader from the Biblical Archaeological Review* (New York: Random House, 1992).

Stegemann, Hartmut, *The Library of Qumran: On the Essenes, Qumran, John the Baptist and Jesus* (Grand Rapids, Mich.: Wm. B. Eerdmans Publishing Co., 1998).

Sussmann, Ayala and Ruth Peled, eds., *Scrolls from the Dead Sea: An Exhibition of Scrolls and Archeological Artifacts from the Collections of the Israel Antiquities Authority* (Washington, D.C.: Library of Congress in association with the Israel Antiquities Authority, 1993).

Talmon, Shemaryahu, "A Calendrical Document from Qumran Cave 4 (Mishmarot D, 4Q325)," in *Solving Riddles and Untying Knots: Biblical, Epigraphic, and Semitic Studies in Honor of Jonas C. Greenfield*, ed. by Ziony Zevit, Seymour Gitin and Michael Sokoloff (Winona Lake, Ind: Eisenbrauns, 1995).

Talmon, Shemaryahu, *The World of Qumran from Within: Collected Studies* (Jerusalem: Magnes Press, The Hebrew University; Leiden: E.J. Brill, c1989).

Tov, Emanuel, "Tefillin of Different Origin from Qumran," in *A Light for Jacob*, ed. by Yair Hoffman and Frank W. Polak (Jerusalem: Bialik Institute, 1997).

Ulrich, Eugene, *The Dead Sea Scrolls and the Origins of the Bible* (Grand Rapids, Mich.: Wm. B. Eerdmans Publishing Co., 1999).

Ulrich, Eugene, and James C. VanderKam, eds., *The Community of the Renewed Covenant: The Notre Dame Symposium on the Dead Sea Scrolls* (Notre Dame, Ind.: University of Notre Dame Press, c1994).

VanderKam, James C., *Calendars in the Dead Sea Scrolls: Measuring Time* (London; New York: Routledge Press, 1998).

VanderKam, James C., *The Dead Sea Scrolls Today* (Grand Rapids, Mich.: Wm. B. Eerdmans Publishing Co., 1994).

VanderKam, James C., *From Revelation to Canon: Studies in the Hebrew Bible and Second Temple Literature* (Leiden: E.J. Brill, 2000).

VanderKam, James C., *The Meaning of the Dead Sea Scrolls: Their Significance for Understanding the Bible, Judaism, Jesus, and Christianity* (San Francisco, Calif.: Harper San Francisco, 2002).

Yadin, Yigael, *The Message of the Scrolls*, ed. by James H. Charlesworth (New York: Crossroad, 1992).

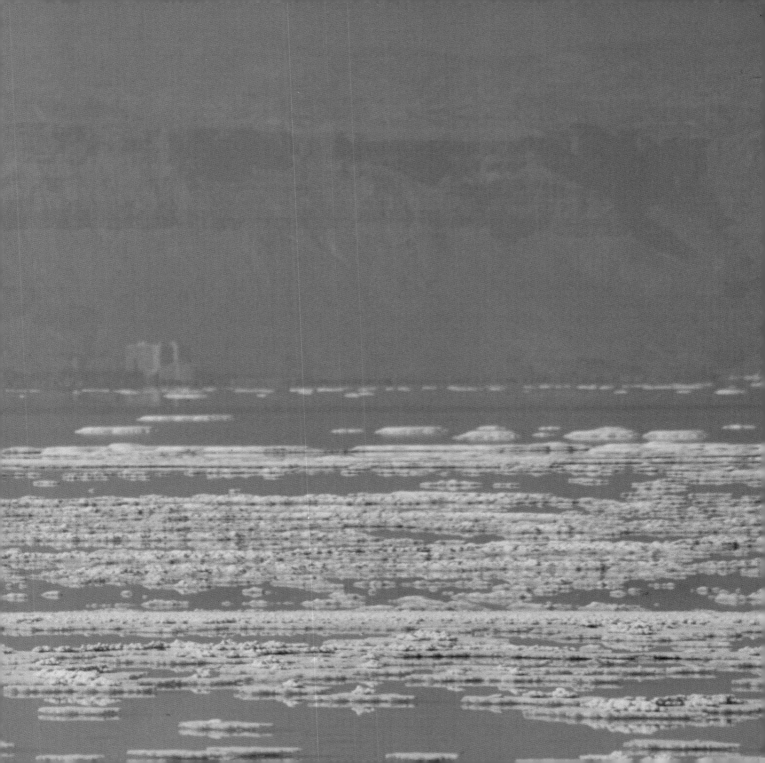

Acknowledgments

The Public Museum of Grand Rapids and Wm. B. Eerdmans Publishing Company would like to acknowledge that this catalog is based in part on *Dead Sea Scrolls* (Sydney, NSW, Australia: Art Gallery of New South Wales, 2000), a catalog produced to accompany an exhibition of Dead Sea Scrolls and artifacts at the Art Gallery of New South Wales, Australia, 14 July – 15 October 2000, and at the National Gallery of Victoria, Australia, in early 2001. The text describing the scrolls and artifacts and the essay "Treasures From the Judean Desert" herein have been taken directly from that catalog with the permission of the Israel Antiquities Authority. This text has occasionally been edited to make it more readable to an American audience.

With the exception of Exodus and Psalms, transcriptions and translations of scroll text are taken from Florentino Garcia Martinez and Eibert J.C. Tigchelaar, *The Dead Sea Scrolls Study Edition*, 2 vols. (Leiden: E.J. Brill; Grand Rapids, Michigan: Wm. B. Eerdmans, 1997, 1998), Transcriptions of Exodus and Psalms are from the Discoveries in the Judaean Desert series. Except where otherwise indicated, translations of all biblical texts are taken from Wayne A. Meeks, et al., with the Society of Biblical Literature, eds., *The HarperCollins Study Bible: New Revised Standard Version, with the Apocryphal/Deuterocanonical Books* (New York: HarperCollins, 1993).

Illustration Credits

Scroll photographs on pages 51, 55, 59, 63, 67, 71, 75, 78-79, 83, 87, 91, 94-95 are used by courtesy of Tsila Sagiv, Israel Antiquities Authority, © IAA.

Artifact photographs on pages 103, 105, 106, 107, 108, 109, 111, 112, 113, 115, 117, 118, 119, 121, 123 are used by courtesy of Clara Amit and Mariana Salzberger, Israel Antiquities Authority, © IAA.

Photographs on pages 6, 10, 18, 40, 101, 124 are used courtesy of the Israel Antiquities Authority, © IAA.

Photographs on pages xii, xviii-1, 23, 24-25, 26, 48, 98, 138-39 are © Phoenix Data Systems (Joel and Neal Bierling) and are used by permission.

Site diagram on page 100 based on a similar diagram in *Dead Sea Scrolls* (Sydney, NSW, Australia: Art Gallery of New South Wales, 2000).

Front Cover Photograph: War Rule Scroll, used by courtesy of Tsila Sagiv, Israel Antiquities Authority, © IAA. Artwork © DDM

Back Cover Photograph © Phoenix Data Systems (Joel and Neal Bierling). Used by permission.